THE PERFORMANCE
PARADOX

THE PERFORMANCE PARADOX

Understanding the Real Drivers that
Critically Affect Outcomes

Jerry L. Harbour

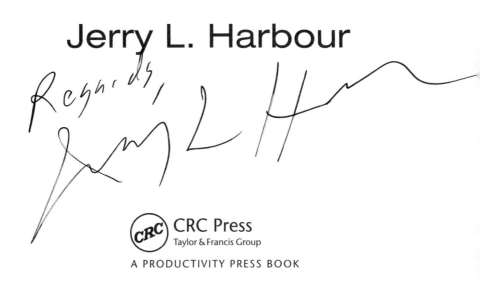

CRC Press
Taylor & Francis Group

A PRODUCTIVITY PRESS BOOK

Productivity Press
Taylor & Francis Group
270 Madison Avenue
New York, NY 10016

© 2009 by Taylor & Francis Group, LLC
Productivity Press is an imprint of Taylor & Francis Group, an Informa business

No claim to original U.S. Government works
Printed in the United States of America on acid-free paper
10 9 8 7 6 5 4 3 2 1

International Standard Book Number-13: 978-1-56327-390-2 (Hardcover)

Library of Congress Cataloging-in-Publication Data

Harbour, Jerry L.
    The performance paradox : understanding the real drivers that critically affect outcomes / Jerry L. Harbour.
        p. cm.
    Includes bibliographical references and index.
    ISBN 978-1-56327-390-2 (1-56327-390-x : alk. paper)
    1. Performance--Measurement. 2. Performance standards. 3. Creative ability in business. 4. Organizational effectiveness. I. Title.

HF5549.5.P37H37 2009
658.3'125--dc22   2008012034

Visit the Taylor & Francis Web site at
http://www.taylorandfrancis.com

and the Productivity Press Web site at
http://www.productivitypress.com

For our grandchildren.

Contents

Introduction

We have all been asked questions that we cannot answer. Yet perhaps more disconcerting is being asked a question that we have never even thought about before, and yet once posed, we realize that we should have considered it ourselves long ago. I found myself in this situation a few years ago when I was asked how performance actually does and does not improve. Much to my surprise and admitted embarrassment, I had never really even thought about the question or posed it myself. Although I have certainly thought long and hard about the question of how to improve performance, I had never actually pondered the question of how performance improves.

A bit chagrined, I immediately embarked on a sort of Don Quixotic journey trying to answer this simple, yet elusive and relatively unexplored question. The journey to date has consumed much of my time over the past few years and has resulted in a couple of published articles describing some initial findings. (The articles were published with the gracious assistance of two esteemed colleagues and good personal friends, Drs. Julie Marble and Harold Blackman.) This book is the result of that journey.

In the following chapters, I attempt to explore this somewhat misunderstood subject of performance. The book strives to better understand varying measures of performance, or what Mark Twain bemused as "lies, damn lies, and statistics." It seeks, above all else, to assist you in finding what is true—that is, what is known and what is not known about performance, what needs to be known, what is useful, and what is not. And it also exposes hype and fad and helps you embrace fact and reality.

Whether you are an optimist or a pessimist, you will find something in the following pages. There is both good news and bad news. There is both hope and disillusionment.

Sprinkled throughout the ensuing pages, you will also find sage and practical advice, which can be translated into concrete action irrespective of your intended area of application.

So, how is this book, *The Performance Paradox*, crafted? It follows the dictates of what psychologists call "declarative and procedural knowledge." *Declarative knowledge* is about knowledge and is theoretical in nature. Conversely, *procedural knowledge* is how-to knowledge. Humans, as a rule, regularly translate "about" knowledge into "how-to" knowledge.

The Performance Paradox follows this same translational process and is divided into two major sections: an "about" first section and a second "how-to" section. The first section, comprised of Chapters 1 through 4, builds upon a succession of basic performance themes, which provide a greater understanding of the fundamental DNA of performance. These basic theme chapters cover a conceptual overview about performance, treating the subject of performance as a subject in and of itself.

In the second section, the information from the first section is translated into a how-to part comprised of Chapters 5 to 7. These chapters cover modeling, measuring, and improving performance, respectively. The practical implications of the first part are illustrated in the second. Finally, Chapter 8 ties everything together in a succinct and concise summary.

I suggest that you pursue *The Performance Paradox* the old-fashioned way, reading one chapter at a time in sequential order. I hope that such a progression will translate the first part's theoretical knowledge into the practical knowledge in the second part.

One final cautionary note is in order. Increasingly, readers shy away from books that do not specifically address their particular areas of interest or that venture outside of a particular discipline, industry, business, or organizational affiliation. Dr. David Woods, a professor at Ohio State University who spends much of his time studying how organizational systems fail, calls this somewhat myopic phenomenon "distancing by differencing"—that is, how we distance ourselves from things that at first appear to be different.

The good news is that once we actually decide to treat the subject of performance as a subject, a number of basic principles and natural laws emerge. Principles and laws that have universal application across diverse subjects that can explain a number of phenomena: from why Apple, the Oakland Athletics, and Iraqi insurgents are so successful to why the improvement in the speed of thoroughbred racehorses, human sprinters, and internal combustion engine speedboats is currently in somewhat of a stall mode.

It is this foundational understanding that fills the following pages. This foundation is continuously coupled with numerous real-world examples of how such ideas have and can be applied. This foundation also addresses the sage advice offered by authors Steven Levitt and Stephen Dubner in their incredible book entitled *Freakonomics:* "It is well and good to opine or theorize about a subject, as humankind is wont to do, but when moral posturing is replaced by an honest assessment of the data, the result is often a new, surprising insight."

So now you can begin this search for surprising insights. And do enjoy!

The Author

Dr. Jerry Harbour combines over 30 years of domestic and international experience from such diverse fields as offshore oil exploration, underground mining, national laboratory research and development, technology start-up, defense and national security, and training. He is the author of three previous books: *The Basics of Performance Measurement*, *Cycle Time Reduction*, and *The Process Reengineering Workbook*. Jerry and his wife, along with their golden retriever, make their home in New Mexico.

Chapter 1

Seeking What Is True

We humans like to make assumptions. Because our assumptions seem to make sense, they often, over time, morph into what we call common sense. Accordingly, opinions become facts. Wrongs become rights. And we profess to intuitively know what is true.

Business executives and others who invest in research and development, for example, know that the key to ever-greater discoveries and technological breakthroughs is ever-greater amounts of investment capital. That is, the size of R&D investment drives R&D success. Return on innovation investment is directly proportional to investment size. Bigger really is better.

Military commanders are no different. They often seem to think with more expensive, technologically advanced, smart, and information- and network-centric weapon systems, they can more easily and successfully defeat their lower-tech and poorer-equipped enemies. In military speak, high-tech is "in-tech."

Public health officials often assume that the more we spend on per capita healthcare, the longer folks will live. Life expectancy is thus directly linked to the quality of medical care. Better medical care in turn is directly tied to ever-greater levels of healthcare spending.

Many in higher education assume that the more we move to e-learning and other high-tech, computer- and software-based instructional systems, the more college students can and will learn. Online is thus rapidly becoming the preferred line. And traditional college classroom teaching involving a talking head is increasingly being viewed as little more than an old, low-tech equivalent.

Sports fans, players, coaches, and managers alike have, through the decades, held strong beliefs about what does and does not drive team performance. Such beliefs often have a life of their own, quickly becoming proven and accepted facts until someone steps up to the plate and convincingly disproves them otherwise.

Most owners of sports teams, for example, earnestly believe that the greater the size of their respective payrolls, the greater the probability of a winning season. For proof, just look at the money that the New York Yankees spends on its players. And do remember that the Yanks won the World Series four out of five seasons from 1996 to 2000. To ensure this ever-increasing trend in spending and supposed salary-linked World Series outcome, the Yankees' payroll continues to be significantly larger than the average team's payroll in Major League Baseball.

Checking Our Assumptions

The list of such examples could be almost endless, but the basic assumption is essentially the same. The more we invest in something—or the more advanced, high-tech, or next-generation something is—the greater the improvement we can realize in something else. Using such logic, more of one thing almost always leads to or drives more of another thing, whether it is a new R&D breakthrough, a World Series title, a longer life, or a resounding military victory. And in all cases, the supposed reasoning for the outcome is essentially the same.

That is our basic assertion. And it is this often strongly held assumption that drives our investments in trying to improve performance irrespective of specific domain, venue, application, or organizational affinity. Although we may say it in different ways, the basic premise is essentially the same: more of one thing begets more of another thing. The two are obviously linked. As one thing goes up, so surely must the other.

Yet is this supposed reality correct? Upon greater scrutiny, is the assumption that more of one thing begets more of another thing actually true? Are such assumptions fact based or merely opinion based? Or are they performance paradoxes, that, upon closer examination, are at odds with what we intuitively seem to know to be true? A *paradox* is an opinion or statement that is contrary to commonly accepted wisdom. It is a declaration or proposition that at first may seem to be absurd or self-contradictory, but in reality expresses a factual truth. In turn, a *performance paradox* is a paradox that refers to what does and does not drive performance. Or as we will learn, what does and does not result in a particular result. Such performance-related paradoxes abound. Let us consider just a few.

R&D Spending

You know the importance of R&D and its role in helping private companies, governmental organizations, and even whole countries stay ahead of the competition. You also assume that the more your company spends on R&D, the greater the results that will accrue and the more competitive the company's position becomes.

A July 2005 *Fortune* magazine article reinforces this commonly held assertion when it notes that "U.S. spending on R&D will also have to increase if the country wants to remain technologically dominant." From such a statement, sound logic seems to dictate that the greater the R&D investment, the greater the return on that investment.

The consulting firm of Booz Allen Hamilton took a systematic and rigorous look at this strongly held belief. The firm studied the supposed importance of R&D spend rate in its Global 1000 Innovation Study, by plotting spend rate versus actual outcomes, such as increases in corporate sales growth. The sample population for the study consisted of the top one thousand global spenders in the private R&D sector.

As described in a fascinating article subtitled "Money Isn't Everything" by Barry Jaruzelski, Kevin Dehoff, and Rakesh Bordia, the study found "few statistical relationships between R&D spend and business results." The article further notes that there is "no discernible relationship between spending levels and most measures of business success."

Although a certain level of R&D spending appears critical, additional spending beyond that necessary figure seems to buy little, if any, actual gain in business success, no matter how one may attempt to measure it. In the case of R&D spending, more does not necessarily transform into better.

Healthcare and Life Expectancy

The same is apparently true in describing the relationship between healthcare spend rate and life expectancy. On a per capita basis and normalized to U.S. dollars, Cuba spends a little over $200 per year on healthcare, according to an annually published United Nations report on human development. The United States, in contrast, spends over $5,000. One would think that such a large disparity in healthcare spending must surely translate into folks in the United States living significantly longer than those residing on the island of Cuba.

Yet, paradoxically, life expectancy is essentially the same in both countries. One can live on the island, drink rum, and smoke good Cuban cigars, and still live as long as someone in the United States. How can this observation possibly be true? Turns out, life expectancy is primarily governed by three basic factors, as described in Chapter 2. And it costs a country about $200 on an average per capita basis to successfully address these three critical drivers that determine how long people live.

Bombing Precision

Here's another example: In the first Gulf War, CNN frequently showed grainy video footage of cockpit displays recording precision strikes by so-called smart bombs or precision-guided munitions (PGMs). Such intelligently guided munitions, flown by equally technologically advanced and stealthy aircraft like the F-117, could be seen piercing the roofs of targeted buildings with almost surgical precision.

The intended target, at least on television, was always completely destroyed (that is, one smart bomb equaled one demolished building), while surrounding buildings were left unscathed. From such displayed footage, the general public believed that the Gulf War was ushering in a new era of smart bombing, an era that must surely relegate so-called unguided dumb bombs to an obscure and distant past. The Department of Defense and its affiliated military contractors, of course, earnestly espoused and propagated this perception.

A General Accounting Office (GAO) report, published in 1997 and based on an earlier and now mostly declassified study, however, took exception to this commonly held high-tech, intelligent-bomb perception.

The GAO report found "no apparent link between the cost of the aircraft and munitions, whether high or low, and their performance in Desert Storm." It further pointed out that both DOD and contractors proffered performance-related claims that, upon critical review and analysis, could not be independently verified or substantiated.

The GAO-published report does not, however, imply that high-tech, stealthy aircraft and precision-guided munitions did not perform well in the first Gulf War. It simply states that their lower-tech and supposedly dumber and cheaper counterparts performed equally well. According to the report, there were no empirically substantiated real or significant differences identified between these two tech extremes in terms of either cost-to-benefit ratio or calculated performance outcomes.

The terrorist organization al-Qaeda may have learned a thing or two from the GAO's published report. In reference to the relatively low-tech and ubiquitous man-portable, shoulder-fired rocket-propelled grenade (RPG), al-Qaeda seems to have considered carefully the cost-to-benefit ratio and resultant performance outcome proposition of this popular weapon. The terrorist organization describes the RPG as the most celebrated of countermeasure weapons.

The RPG is essentially a grenade fired or propelled from an iron tube by a small rocket. Originally developed by the Germans during World War II, the RPG was later adapted by the Soviets as an anti-armor weapon. According to a captured al-Qaeda training manual referenced in an open article published in the Jamestown Foundation's *Terrorism Monitor*, the RPG,

> costing tens of dollars, can destroy a 100 million dollar tank! And two of them can destroy two tanks! There is simply no relation between the volume of loss and the effort or cost expended to achieve this loss. The fact of the matter is that countermeasures in general, and RPGs in particular, are a blessing granted by God to guerrilla fighters. They [guerrillas] do not possess the machinery or tanks that remain vulnerable to these countermeasures, while the enemy is incapable of functioning without this machinery—which permits a target that couldn't be more ideal.

Irrespective of the perceived social acceptability of the quoted source, one can still learn a great deal from this performance-based insight. Indeed, as I am writing this chapter, the U.S. military is facing an ever-growing insurgency in Iraq. Many in the United States and abroad are questioning how such a supposedly low-tech, insurgency-based threat can, if not outright beat, then at least effectively compete against America's high-tech weaponry might, which currently costs U.S. taxpayers a shade over $500 billion per year.

Perhaps the words of retired Major General Robert Scales, a former commander of the Army War College, offer some prudent insights. Scales argues that there is "no appreciable technological advantage for an American infantryman when fighting the close battle against even the poorest, most primitive enemy." To underscore his point, he notes that since the end of World War II, every four out of five American combat fatalities have been infantrymen, even though infantrymen constitute less than 5 percent of all servicemen. Argues Scales, infantrymen do "virtually all the killing and dying."

Currently, Iraqi insurgents and U.S.-led forces are fighting this close battle in the crowded streets and cities of Iraq, especially Baghdad. And, consequently, America's military technological might is being effectively negated. Although Iraqi insurgents have not gained a technological superiority over the Americans, they have nevertheless achieved a certain performance parity of sorts. The enabling mechanics behind achieving such performance parity, often at significantly lower costs, is discussed more fully in Chapter 5.

e-Learning

In a final example, many universities have eagerly and expensively embraced the computer age in an attempt to enhance student learning. Asynchronous, computer-based e-learning is the current trend in higher education. Additionally, software-based learning tools are increasingly being used in elementary and secondary classrooms, especially in an attempt to enhance reading and mathematical skills. But does all of this high-tech instructional technology actually improve learning? According to a recently released study by the National Center for Education and Regional Assistance, an arm of the U.S. Department of Education, the answer is no.

The study assesses the learning efficacy of sixteen instructional software products that were grouped into four areas: first grade reading, fourth grade reading, sixth grade math, and general algebra courses. Thirty-three school districts involving 132 schools and 439 teachers took part in the study. Within each school, teachers were randomly assigned to using the software products (the treatment group) or not (the control group). For the treatment groups, most teachers received prior training on using the software products, and after the training, they self-reported that they felt prepared to use the new instructional software technology in their classrooms.

To determine learning effects, tests were administered to students in both types of classrooms near the beginning and end of the school year. Corresponding improvements in learning, as indicated by gains from beginning to end of school year tests, were analyzed and statistically compared between treatment and control groups.

According to the report released in April 2007 entitled *Effectiveness of Reading and Mathematics Software Products: Findings from the First Student Cohort*, the study found that

> test scores were not higher by statistically significant margins in classrooms using selected reading and mathematics software products than in those classrooms that didn't use such products.

It is perhaps important and only fair to note, however, that despite such non-significant findings, most teachers in the treatment group stated that they would use the instructional software products again, even in the presence of some minor technical problems they encountered along the way.

Like the GAO report comparing smart bombs and dumb bombs, no statistically significant differences were found between classrooms using high-tech versus good-old teacher-tech. Although you may be dismayed by such education findings, especially in this technology-based era, perhaps all of us, irrespective of our individual tech passions, should heed the sage advice and "law" of Jeffrey Pfeffer, professor of organizational behavior at Stanford's Graduate School of Business. Pfeffer's law states that "instead of being interested in what is new, we ought to be interested in what is true."

Dollars Spent Equals Games Won

But surely there must be some closely held truths that are indeed fact based—aren't there? Perhaps it is the New York Yankee–referenced correlation between team payroll size and team success that we can look to. After all, Major League Baseball established a blue-ribbon panel in 1999 to investigate payroll inequities in professional baseball. Specifically, the panel sought to "examine the question of whether Baseball's current economic system has created a problem of competitive imbalance in the game."

The ensuing panel's report, published in 2000 under the title of "The Report of the Independent Members of the Commissioner's Blue Ribbon Panel on Baseball Economics," did indeed find payroll discrepancies over the years that the report covered (from 1995 to 1999).

The panel's findings seem to make sense. Do not forget, one only has to look at the performance of the New York Yankees during much of the investigated interval to see that they won the series in 1996, 1998, 1999, and 2000. Over those same years, except in 1998, the Yanks had the highest payroll in baseball. When they won the title in 1998, they still had the second-highest payroll in baseball.

As such, the "undeniable evidence" collected by the panel should seem obvious to almost anyone. Payroll size really does matter! Just ask Bob Costas, author of *Fair Ball: A Fan's Case for Baseball*. According to Costas, "The single biggest indicator of a team's opportunity for success from one year to the next is whether the team has a payroll among the top few teams in the league. Period."

Yet not everything may seem as it first appears. In a must-read book entitled *The Wages of Wins* by David Berri, Martin Schmidt, and Stacey Brook, the three university economic professors turned authors take a closer look at the panel's report and resulting conclusions.

Knowing that, in statistics, sample size really does matter, the three professors looked at the years preceding and following the blue-ribbon panel's 1995 to 1999 analytical coverage. In short, they found that by using a larger sample size in terms of years studied, the relationship between payroll size and wins did not confirm the linkage between payroll and World Series titles. In fact, between 1989 and 1993, baseball teams in the third quartile of payroll size won the series almost half of the time. In the years from 2000 to 2004, fourth quartile teams or the lowest-paid teams still managed to capture the grand prize of baseball some 14 percent of the time.

And what has happened since to our beloved New York Yankees? The three economic professors note that from "2002 to 2005 the Yankees spent like never before. And after all that spending, not a single title did they buy." They didn't buy a title in 2006 or 2007 either.

To be fair, however, it is important to point out that the Yanks made an incredible comeback in 2007 after getting off to a horrible start, ending the season with 94 wins and 68 losses. Yet in the end, the $216 million Yanks lost the opening 2007 division playoffs to the $70.5 million Cleveland Indians, resulting in the resignation of long-time Yankee manager Joe Torre.

In the same division playoffs, the $100.6 million Philadelphia Phillies lost three straight games to the $60.6 million Colorado Rockies, while the $113.5 million Chicago Cubs were swept by the $69.8 million Arizona Diamondbacks. Only the high-dollar Boston Red Sox persevered, ending up winning the World Series against Colorado in four straight games. Just as money may not always buy happiness, it does not always buy a winning baseball team either.

We will return to the game of baseball again when we describe in Chapter 2 how the Oakland Athletics, a consistently successful team with an equally consistent low-dollar payroll, fundamentally rethought the game of baseball relating to what does and does not really matter. It turns out that it is not solely about batting average after all. Rather, it is also about on-base percentage or the probability that a batter will not make an out. Once the Oakland A's recognized this critical performance truth, they began to value and acquire players in a fundamentally different manner, as did many other teams.

Performance Paradoxes

When discussing R&D spend rate, life expectancy, high-tech weaponry, the World Series, or just about anything else, performance-related paradoxes abound. Whether in business, warfare, healthcare, education, or sports, it seems that we hold many assumptions that are believed to be well-known truths. Yet upon closer examination, such apparent truths often do not hold up to fact-based scrutiny. These performance paradoxes often needlessly consume scarce organizational resources—resources that can be better and more effectively spent elsewhere.

Incorrectly held performance-related truths also set up business leaders and investors for disappointment and disillusionment. Often in the end, our recently funded and guaranteed performance improvement silver bullet turns out to be little more than an ordinary lead one, at best.

This does not mean, however, that businesses should lose hope. It just means that you need to take the time to learn a bit more about how performance results actually result, and how you can better identify those key drivers that critically affect performance outcomes. To embark on such a journey, however, you must first begin by better understanding some of the core concepts and precepts of performance.

At the most elemental level, you must understand how performance does and does not improve and why all performance improvement accruals eventually stall out, reaching a performance plateau or asymptote that, with practice, becomes easily recognizable. Once this limiting asymptote is reached, simply doing more of the same does not work, so understanding this reality can often help less bountiful organizations achieve surprising performance parities even among their richer and more powerful competitors.

It is also true that you must understand the realistic limits of performance— what the late and highly gifted professor and author Stephen Jay Gould labeled the "walls of performance." But at the same time, you must also grasp the often beneficial role of innovation in restarting the performance improvement process anew.

It is also important to learn how to better identify factors that do and do not drive performance. For example, most organizations have crafted in some form or another vision and mission statements, yet few organizations have spent equal time or effort crafting a *performance statement*—a succinct summary of those key factors that truly drive organizational success.

The good news is that there are some notable exceptions to this observation, and some organizations have not only identified key performance factors but also further translated them into applicable and actionable performance models and associated metrics. These performance models and metric systems, once created, are continuously tinkered with and studied, and in turn are used to guide much of an organization's tactical and strategic decision-making efforts.

Admittedly, such performance models are far from perfect. They certainly do not or cannot account for or predict everything. And, on occasion, wrong organizational decisions are still made and will continue to be made. Yet even in this admitted state of imperfection, such models seem to be better than anything else around. And in the end, perhaps that is about as good as it gets in this real and imperfect world.

Summary

A paradox is an opinion or statement that is contrary to commonly accepted wisdom. A performance paradox is a paradox that refers to what does and does not drive performance, or what does and does not result in a result. Such paradoxes abound and often needlessly consume scarce organizational resources that could be better and more effectively spent elsewhere. Incorrectly held performance-related truths also set up business leaders and investors for disappointment and disillusionment, as well as drive poor decision making.

Chapter 2

Performance as Subject and Why *x* Matters

Countless books have been written about how to improve performance. Numerous others (including my own *Basics of Performance Measurement*) address the practical application of measuring performance. Yet, surprisingly in this plethora of writing, there is a genuine dearth of books *about* performance—that is, books that have been written solely with the expressed purpose of exploring the subject of performance as, well, a subject.

Defining Performance

It seems that in our haste to codify the technology of performance, we have somehow forgotten to first develop a theoretical basis for that codification. This is somewhat akin to creating the technology of surgery without first taking the time to understand human anatomy, learn where all the body parts are located, and have a sense of how they function and fit together. Accordingly, you begin your initial exploration of performance without attempting to do anything to it (that is, improve or measure it), except simply study and describe it.

To *perform* means to initiate and execute a set of actions (that is, an activity). The translation of these actions into an actual result, outcome, or accomplishment is termed *performance*. Associated performance-related actions are thus the means, whereas the accomplishment is the end result. Performance, therefore, represents something tangible: an end.

The late Thomas Gilbert, performance improvement guru extraordinaire, said it best at a conference I attended when he noted that performance is what is left at the end of the day after everyone has gone home—an actual or concrete accomplishment. Performance in and of itself, however, does not imply merit or value. Performance, good or bad, is still performance. A bad day on the golf course still ends in a result, however disconcerting and upsetting that result may be.

A performance outcome, be it sales volume, points scored in an NBA basketball game, or years lived, is commonly expressed with the letter Y and is plotted on the vertical axis of most performance-related graphs. In turn, those factors or variables that supposedly cause or contribute to outcome Y are often designated with the letter x and are plotted on the horizontal axis of graphs. Y thus represents the *end* and x the *means* of performance. It is critical to understand and measure both the outcome itself *and* the means (or processes) for deriving that outcome.

Developing a Performance Equation

Based on these Y and x symbols, you can write a simple equation describing performance. In short, performance outcome Y can be expressed as a function of variable set x. This expression is often portrayed by the formula $Y = f(x)$.

For example, life expectancy, defined as the average number of years someone can expect to live at birth, is determined primarily by three key factors: infant mortality, defined by the death rate from birth to 1 year of age (sadly, many infant-related deaths occur within the first 24 hours of life); adolescent mortality, defined by the death rate from ages 1 through 5; and maternal mortality, defined by the death rate of mothers during childbirth.

Given these three key x factors or variables, we can now translate them into a $Y = f(x)$ performance formula. Thus, life expectancy (your Y or desired performance outcome) is a function of infant mortality (x_1), adolescent mortality (x_2), and maternal mortality (x_3). This function can be expressed as: life expectancy = f(infant mortality + adolescent mortality + maternal mortality).

Taking the Equation One Step Further

In turn, you may wish to roll up or aggregate life expectancy into some higher-level performance outcome. This is exactly what the United Nations did when it developed its Human Development Index (HDI). The UN defines HDI as a "summary measure of human development." HDI attempts to measure average human development achievements irrespective of a particular country along three basic dimensions:

- A *long and healthy life*, as measured by life expectancy at birth
- *Knowledge*, as measured by adult literacy rate (representing a two-thirds weighting) and the combined primary, secondary, and tertiary gross school enrollment ratios (representing a one-third weighting)
- A *decent standard of living*, as measured by per capita gross domestic product (GDP), normalized to U.S. dollar equivalents

You can now write a new formula that portrays HDI as a function of (life expectancy) + (adult literacy + combined primary, secondary, and tertiary gross school enrollment ratio) + (GDP).

Although calculating an actual human development index is a bit more complicated, the real challenge in such measures is developing the underlying logic, identifying the important x variables that truly affect performance and the relationships between and among those key variables.

Understanding the Three Types of x Variables

There are three basic types of x variables:

- Those that significantly affect performance in a positive manner
- Those that significantly affect performance in a negative manner
- Those that have little or no real effect on performance

The key is trying to identify which is which, identifying those variables that are truly important and understanding how they are important, and identifying and understanding those variables that really are not important at all.

Imagine for a moment that you want to purchase a new oceangoing container or so-called box ship. Before spending such a significant amount of money, however, you first want to create a performance-based formula that effectively identifies those few important factors that critically affect profitability.

After thinking about the problem for awhile, you decide that you will make money only when you are transporting revenue-generating cargo across the ocean. This is a key *positive* factor. You lose money, however, when you are in port, either waiting to be unloaded or actually being unloaded or reloaded. This is a key *negative* factor. The color of your ship, however, has no bearing on potential profitability.

Armed with such knowledge, you can now create an admittedly simplistic performance formula that states: profitability = time cargo-filled vessel is under way – time in port.

Successfully identifying those next lower-level factors that in turn comprise the "time the cargo-filled vessel is under way" and the "time in port" represents your next challenge. Yet knowing this simple beginning equation according to Marc Levinson, author of *The Box: How the Shipping Container Made the World Smaller and the World Economy Bigger*, makes the "time in port" side of the equation relatively straightforward. Levinson notes that developing the equation "was simple: the bigger the port, the bigger the vessels it could handle and the faster it could empty them, reload them, and send them back to sea."

Thinking, however, that you might not want to purchase a container ship after all but instead field an America's Cup racing sailboat, you now become interested in identifying a new set of critical performance factors.

America's Cup boats are often called the Formula 1's of the sea. They are built with a single purpose in mind: speed. The boats field a crew of seventeen, plus one guest during a race. Fitted with a single mast rigged to hold some 7,500 square feet of main and spinnaker sails made of Kevlar, carbon fiber, and Mylar (note that a basketball court contains only 4,700 square feet), the 24-ton boats particularly like the downwind leg of the America's Cup race course, which may be as long as 12.6 nautical miles. The carbon-fiber-made hulls, some six times as long as wide, can slice through the water in both up- and downwind directions at overall speeds averaging 15 to 16 knots (17 to 18 miles per hour).

America's Cup boats are also heavily instrumented and monitored. On-board computers can measure a number of variables, including water and air pressure, velocity, and boat motion. In fact, some of the more high-tech boats collect and display over two hundred measurements every second. Although no outside communications are allowed *to* a boat during a race, collected data can be transmitted to shore-based technicians who analyze and store the transmitted data in massive databases.

After conducting a bit of research, you learn that a type of performance pyramid has already been developed for competitive sailing. At the bottom of the pyramid sits *boat handling*, including things like the time that it takes a crew to change sails or to tack from one direction to another. In the middle of the pyramid sits *boat speed*, primarily controlled by things like hull shape, hull material construction, and sail configuration.

At the top sits *tactics* that relate to overall racing strategy and navigation. This latter, tactics-related pyramid category represents the crew's brain trust or, in nautical terms, the *after guard*. The after guard primarily consists of the *tactician*, who decides when to tack or jibe; the *strategist*, who continuously monitors wind and weather conditions; and the *navigator*, who determines the best course to take based on continuing updates and inputs from the tactician and strategist.

Therefore, whether you are dealing with massive container ships or sleek America's Cup racing sailboats, desired outcomes are often driven by only a few key factors. Such factors, if properly identified, can often increase the probability of success, whether that success is determined by boat profitability or boat speed.

To briefly summarize, performance represents an outcome, accomplishment, or result. Outcomes expressed by the letter Y are a function of a set of key variables expressed by the letter x. Accordingly, Y is a function of variable set x or $Y = f(x)$.

Adding Oomph to Your Performance Equation

Although many variables can potentially affect a performance outcome in either a positive or negative direction, what we are really interested in is identifying those key factors that have a truly significant effect on Y. This means identifying those factors that, according to economist Deirde McClosky, not only are statistically significant but also add true oomph to your performance equation. For McCloskey, oomph factors are what matter most.

In the following sections, I help you explore how others identify critical oomph factors. I will begin this exploration by describing how those in the military logistics business calculate the number of aircraft needed to transport a set amount of cargo in a single operational day. Specifically, in this example, you can calculate how many aircraft are required to resupply a group of Marines that has taken an objective 100 nautical miles from offshore-based amphibious support ships. Although some might view the world of logistics as more art than science, it is in reality a discipline that is very much based on quantification: How much? How far? How fast? How long?

Next, I will turn to baseball. The good thing about sports, and particularly baseball, is that you have lots of numbers to work with. Every day a game is played, people are recording all sorts of performance-related measures. For this baseball-related discussion I rely primarily on three great books: *Moneyball* by Michael Lewis; *The Book—Playing the Percentages in Baseball* by Tom Tango, Mitchel Lichtman, and Andrew Dolphin; and *Baseball Between the Numbers*, edited by Jonah Keri.

After spending a bit of time identifying key performance factors in baseball, I will next move to the world of landmines and unexploded ordnance, summarizing an insightful article written by Colonel Alastair McAslan and Keith Feigenbaum that was published in James Madison University's *Journal of Mine Action*. What is so informative about the authors' published work is their use of a simple graph that vividly and understandably captures the essence of their performance-related threat formula.

Although few people directly make a living in military logistics, professional sports, or landmines and unexploded ordnance (UXO), the underlying logic presented in these three examples—and how that logic is developed—represents the real message. The same type of logic construction can be successfully applied to many other domains as well.

Remember, the critical challenge in constructing a performance-based formula is not necessarily the math, which, in many instances, is actually quite simple. Rather, it is the underlying logic that results in the math. As you will see, it is this underlying logic that represents the real essence in understanding the DNA of performance. After you discover that logic, you can then develop performance measures to quantitatively capture the truly important.

From Sea to Land

Historians like to portray a vision of a bunch of fierce Mongrel warriors, mounted on horseback, swooping out of the barren steppes of northern Asia at lightning speed, pillaging and plundering helpless armies and villagers alike. Although the warriors comprising Genghis Khan's massive armies were certainly fierce and mounted on horseback, it is highly doubtful that they did their swooping at lightning speed.

In fact, Khan's armies moved fairly slowly in their quest to dominate the Eurasian landscape, progressing only some 5 miles per day at best. It turned out that when Mongrel warriors decided to go to war, each warrior liked to take a number of things along with them, including five horses (one for riding and four for grazing), his wife, and his children.

Taking along the family necessitated also taking along a large number of goats, sheep, and oxen, as well as a ger (tent) and all required ger furnishings. Khan must have learned quickly what every other military leader has been forced to learn since: moving lots of stuff can take lots of time and require lots of transport vehicles. In this regard, not much has really changed, even in today's fairly high-tech military.

A primary role of the U.S. Marines, for example, is to be able to maneuver from the sea, moving troops and supplies quickly from offshore amphibious ships stationed 25 miles out at sea to an inland objective. Ideally, in such scenarios, vertical takeoff and landing (VTOL) aircraft are used, thereby allowing Marines to bypass the deadly beach zone and move troops and supplies directly inland to an assigned objective.

Ship-based helicopters have historically been used to transport troops and required supplies. The Marines, however, are currently in the process of introducing the MV-22 Osprey, a hybrid tilt-rotor aircraft, to perform such ship-to-land transport missions.

The Osprey certainly is a unique aircraft, representing a hybrid between a helicopter and an airplane. When the Osprey's large propeller blades face upward, it can take off and land vertically like a helicopter. Once airborne, however, the propellers on each side of the twin-engine craft rotate forward 90 degrees, allowing the Osprey to convert to a plane.

Although technologically unique, the Osprey has unfortunately been plagued by a number of safety issues and resultant deadly accidents. It has also had considerable trouble successfully meeting requisite programmatic operational goals, or what are termed key performance parameters. Additionally, proffered (and perhaps somewhat overstated) contractor promises have, to date, failed to be fully realized.

Putting aside such problems for a moment, you can still attempt to perform a simplistic analysis, comparing mission performance capability between the futuristic MV-22 Osprey and the Marine's currently employed CH-53E Super Stallion heavy lift helicopter. But to undertake such a comparison, you first need a logistics-based performance model or formula. In this comparative example, you are interested in only determining *logistics productivity*, or how much cargo can be moved as measured by tons of material transported per day, along with the respective number of aircraft needed to support the required supply mission.

Logistics productivity as it relates to moving cargo by helicopter and tilt-rotor aircraft is dependent on three primary oomph factors:

- The number of mission aircraft that can be kept functioning throughout the day
- The mission load as measured in pounds that can be carried on each round-trip flight (called a sortie)
- The number of mission sorties that each aircraft can fly in a given operational day

Based on these three critical factors, you can create a general logistics productivity formula that states our $Y = f(x)$ proposition as: tons per day = mission aircraft × mission tons per sortie × mission sorties per aircraft per day.

Before comparing the two aircraft, however, a bit more explanation is necessary. The number of aircraft that can be kept operating during a mission is a function of the number of aircraft assigned to the mission, adjusted by an average availability factor. Unfortunately, aircraft break down. Accordingly, it is often necessary to have more aircraft assigned to a critical military transport mission than will actually be flying, because some aircraft will almost certainly be in a state of disrepair and unable to fly. If you need eight aircraft to complete a given mission, for example, and you are using an 80 percent availability factor, you actually need ten aircraft to successfully complete the mission (80 percent × 10 aircraft = 8 aircraft).

In calculating *mission load* (or tons per sortie), a number of factors must be considered. First, for helicopters and tilt-rotor aircraft, there is an inverse relationship between useful load or the amount of cargo that can actually be carried and fuel. As one goes up, the other goes down: more fuel means less cargo, whereas more cargo means less fuel.

Additionally, and as learned during the first Gulf War, a cargo aircraft will normally "cube out" before it maxes out on weight. Cargo volume (or shape) is thus a bigger load-determining factor than weight, except for fairly compact cargo loads like fuel and ammunition. As such, stated maximum load ratings have little practical value. For realistic planning purposes, maximum loads are almost always reduced, sometimes significantly so.

The number of sorties per aircraft per day is a function of the time it takes to load and offload troops and supplies, aircraft turnaround time, aircraft speed, and length of allowable flight hours in an operational day (usually 10 or 12 hours, if restricted by daylight). Note that although a tilt-rotor aircraft like the MV-22 has a much faster cruise speed than a helicopter (in other words, it can fly faster: 240 knots versus 130 knots), on shorter-distance operations involving moving cargo only from offshore to a relatively close inland destination, such speed advantages are often negated by requisite loading and turnaround times.

You can now make the comparison. Assume that the Marines are currently holding an inland objective 100 nautical miles from offshore-positioned amphibious ships and are desperately in need of additional supplies. The total weight of needed supplies equals 200 tons. Further assume that you have a 12-hour operational flight day and an 80 percent aircraft availability factor (some might argue that this figure is actually too high for the MV-22 based on current operational testing results). Finally, for calculation purposes, assume that the CH-53E helicopter can transport 20,000 pounds per sortie and the MV-22 can transport 5,000 pounds (note that these numbers are rounded off a bit high, but not by much).

Using the tons per day formula presented earlier, you can make some rough calculations comparing mission performance of the two aircraft. Assume you are particularly interested in determining how many respective aircraft are required to successfully complete the required mission: How many MV-22s and CH-53Es are needed?

For the MV-22 Osprey, your calculation will look like this: 200 tons per day = 15 aircraft × 5,000 lb per sortie × 6.55 mission sorties per aircraft per day.

Your calculation for the CH-53E helicopter is: 200 tons per day = 7 aircraft × 20,000 lb per sortie × 4.50 mission sorties per aircraft per day.

From this example (although a bit oversimplified), it appears that you will need about twice as many MV-22s to complete the mission as compared to CH-53Es (fifteen MV-22s versus seven CH-53Es). In this mission-specific example, the greater load-carrying capacity of the CH-53E helicopter is much more decisive from a mission performance perspective than the greater cruise speed of the MV-22 Osprey.

Of course, other factors must be taken into account as well: aircraft-related safety, survivability, cost, and so on. Yet even from this brief illustration, you can easily understand why the high-cost Osprey has generated so much controversy among safety-, mission-, and budget-conscious foes.

The important lesson here, however, is not the specifics of military transport or the MV-22 versus the CH-53E, but rather how you approached this comparative analysis. To summarize the approach, you first created a $Y = f(x)$ formula using three primary determining factors. Then the constructed $Y = f(x)$ model drove the approach, utilized measures, and resultant outcomes. You will use this same basic approach time and again: performance *models* dictate utilized performance *measures* and resultant measured performance *outcomes*.

Small Round Balls That Fly

Every once and awhile, someone pauses and takes a fundamentally new look at something that has been supposedly known for decades. Amateur baseball theorist Bill James did just that.

Years ago, James became convinced that the established conventional wisdom of baseball was not entirely correct. Although most baseball insiders at the time were content to rely on well-established conventional wisdom, James set out in search of what he describes as objective knowledge about baseball. Today this objective knowledge pursuit is known as *sabermetrics*, a name James coined in honor of the Society for American Baseball Research (SABR).

Much of the rethinking in baseball espoused by James and others is captured perfectly in an easy-to-read and nontechnical book entitled *Moneyball* by Michael Lewis. *Moneyball* is a book about using statistics to better understand the secret of success in baseball and how the low-budget Oakland Athletics have consistently applied that understanding in creating winning season after winning season (except, unfortunately, when injuries plagued the team throughout the recent 2007 season).

Our particular interest here, however, is much narrower. It focuses only on a logic statement (or performance model) that is perfectly written in a single succinct paragraph, and the translation of that logic statement into an equally simple and succinct yet powerful mathematical formula. According to Lewis, the Oakland Athletics commissioned Eric Walker, an aerospace engineer turned baseball writer, to write a pamphlet analyzing the game of baseball. Walker captures the essence of what is really important in baseball in the following paragraph:

> Analyzing baseball yields many numbers of interest and value. Yet far and away—far, far and away—the most critical number in all of baseball is 3: the three outs that define an ending. Until the third out, anything is possible; after it, nothing is. Anything that increases the offense's chances of making an out is bad; anything that decreases it is good. And what is on-base percentage? Simply yet exactly put, it is the probability that the batter will not make an out. When we state it that way, it becomes, or should become, crystal clear that the most important isolated one-dimensional offensive statistic is the on-base percentage. It measures the probability that the batter will not be another step toward the end of the inning.

It seems to Walker that what you do when you are up at bat matters most. And what matters most is not making an out!

So how can you prevent an out in baseball? The answer is by getting on base. And how does that happen? Normally by getting either a hit or a walk, or more infrequently and painfully, by getting dinged with an errant or intentional pitch, an event that happens about once in every hundred appearances at the plate.

As stated, the number of times a player reaches base safely without making an out is known as *on-base percentage* (OBP). The formula for OBP is: OBP = (hits + walks + hits by pitch) ÷ (at-bats + walks + hits by pitch + sacrifice flies).

Note that OBP does not differentiate between walks and hits, be it a single, double, triple, or home run. All that OBP attempts to measure is the number of times a player reaches base and the probability that the batter will not make an out.

The quantitative importance of OBP is expertly captured and explained by Tango, Lichtman, and Dolphin in their book entitled *The Book—Playing the Percentages in Baseball*. According to the three authors, at the start of an inning with no outs and with no one on base, on average, a team will score about 0.555 runs before the inning ends. They came up with this 0.555 figure by calculating the average runs scored per inning for the 1999 through 2002 baseball seasons.

If the leadoff hitter (with no outs and no one on base) gets on first base via walk, run, or hit by a pitch, this 0.555 figure increases to 0.953. As such, getting on base is worth an increase in run expectancy, at least theoretically speaking, of 0.398 runs (0.953 − 0.555 = 0.398). Conversely, if the leadoff hitter does not get on base, then run expectancy decreases from the starting 0.555 figure to 0.297, a loss of −0.258.

In short, the more people who get on base regardless of how they do it (keep in mind the importance of OBP), the greater the run expectancy for the inning. And the more runs a team makes per inning, the greater the probability that at the end of the game they will come out on top. Thus, OBP really does matter, both figuratively and literally.

Armed with this new insight about the surprising importance of OBP, the Oakland A's started acquiring players that could not only hit the ball, but also had the discipline to not take a swing at just any old pitch that came across the plate. In essence, these players had better at-bat management skills than many other so-called more desirable players with higher batting averages but often lower on-base percentage numbers.

Further, as it turns out, players with good batting discipline and on-base percentage numbers have another added value. Because they are patient and disciplined when up at the plate, they frequently force the opposing pitcher to throw more pitches. Baseball is really a game of attrition, and what is being "attrited" is a pitcher's arm.

So a better on-base percentage not only translates into being on base more and thus in a better position to score if the opportunity arises, but also can shorten a pitcher's on-mound performance time. If a pitcher is forced to throw more pitches per individual batter appearance, then he's likely to be forced to leave the game earlier, thus forcing a manager to go to his bullpen earlier.

In the end and from such analyses, a deeper and new understanding of the game of baseball emerged. Driven primarily by looking at the numbers of the game of baseball in new statistical or sabermetric ways, greater insights accrued. For example, in addition to identifying the value of on-base percentage, *slugging average*, or the average number of bases gained per individual hit, was also identified as a critical performance variable.

The culmination of these insights is perhaps best evidenced by a *runs created* formula crafted by Bill James. According to James, runs created = (hits + walks) × total bases ÷ (at-bats + walks).

In the book *Moneyball*, Lewis describes James' formula as a "scientific hypothesis: a model that would predict the number of runs a team would score given its walks, steals, singles, doubles, etc."

Lewis further notes that many in professional baseball "didn't place enough value on walks and extra base hits, which featured prominently in the 'Runs Created' model, and placed too much value on batting average and stolen bases, which James didn't even bother to include." In short, by rethinking the logic of the game of baseball and translating that logic into a kind of performance model and associated formula, a whole new understanding emerged. This understanding has, for the Oakland Athletics and many other teams since, fundamentally changed how teams value, acquire, and manage baseball players.

But what about the value of defense, especially pitching and fielding? In *Baseball Between the Numbers*, a book written by the Baseball Prospectus Team of Experts and edited by Jonah Keri, the writers argue that defense—and particularly pitching—is especially important during the playoffs. Because there are really no bad teams in the playoffs, good hitters on the various teams more or less cancel each other out. Thus, the performance of starting pitchers and the bullpen becomes increasingly important in playoff games, as demonstrated by the greater in-depth pitching prowess of the Boston Red Sox against the Colorado Rockies in the 2007 World Series. Although offense still matters, apparently in the playoffs it just does not matter quite as much.

Things That Go Boom

The two examples in the preceding sections illustrate how others have gone about developing the underlying logic of identifying key drivers of wanted performance outcomes, represented by logistics productivity in the first example and runs created in baseball in the second example. We now turn our attention to modeling an unwanted outcome or, in this case, specific factors that increase the risk associated with removing landmines and unexploded ordnance.

Landmines and unexploded ordnance (UXO), often captured under the recently introduced rubric of *explosive remnants of war* (ERW), represent a daunting challenge in postconflict countries. Tragically, the bulk of such problems occur in the less developed parts of the world and serve only to exacerbate an already challenging country condition.

The sheer numbers of the so-called ERW problem are absolutely mind-boggling. Some 60 million landmines alone are thought to litter sixty to seventy countries, causing untold heartache and harm among innocent populations. The Egyptian government, for example, claims that Egypt, one of the most landmine- and UXO-affected countries in the world, is infested with approximately 20 million landmines and UXO. Western Egypt in particular is affected by this deadly menace as a result of a number of major battles fought there during World War II.

Indeed, while the armies of Field Marshall Montgomery and Rommel fought each other in North Africa during the Second World War, millions of anti-tank (AT) and anti-personnel (AP) landmines were buried in defensive positions. The area around the legendary perimeter of El Alamein was so densely seeded with landmines by the armies of Italy, Germany, and England that an estimated 2,900 square kilometers are still considered contaminated with literally millions of mines and remain off limits to human settlement and travel. Even during the war, German Field Marshal Rommel referred to the area as the "gardens of the devil."

Laos represents another tragic example. Between 1964 and 1973, intense ground combat and aerial bombing campaigns associated with the war in Vietnam released approximately 2 million tons of ordnance over Laos. This figure represents an astonishing 2 tons of ordnance for every man, woman, and child living in Laos at the time. And up to 30 percent of that ordnance may have failed to explode, leaving approximately two-thirds of the country, or some 87,000 square kilometers, still contaminated and dangerous today.

In both Laos and Cambodia, small bomblets or cluster munitions dispensed from larger cluster bombs that were dropped during the Vietnam-era conflict continue to exert a tragic toll on countryside villagers. Some 4 million BLU-26 cluster bomblets are thought to currently litter the Laotian landscape and are especially dangerous when found buried in the country's many rice fields.

Because of the sheer size of the problem and the realities of limited resources to effectively deal with it, it is often necessary to first assess and prioritize the nature of the threat posed to a local population living in a specific area. Such assessments normally involve analyzing both risk and cumulative threat. *Risk*, notes McAslan and Feigenbaum, refers to "the probability and severity of a single occurrence of harm." In turn, the *cumulative threat* posed by mines and UXO refers to the sum of local risks present in an area.

Many humanitarian, nongovernment organizations (NGOs) involved in initial ERW assessments and subsequent removal efforts use a threat-based model predicated on four key factors:

■ The *area* affected by landmines and other ERW
■ The physical *properties* of the contamination
■ The *concentration* of the contamination
■ The *impact* on population masses exposed to the threat

These assessments essentially answer the *where, what, how much*, and *who* questions.

McAslan and Feigenbaum present a similar model, although their focus is not on assessing the threat posed to an affected populace, but instead deals with those who must actually remove these deadly gardens of the devil. According to the two authors, in clearing landmines and UXO, the *probability of harm* is a combination of the quantity of munitions with the probability to cause harm, and the probability of failing to detect a single active mine/UXO.

This simple logic statement in turn is composed of three key elements:

- The *type* of landmine- or UXO-associated hazard present (fragmentation, blast, or incendiary) and the severity of physical harm caused by an unintended detonation
- The ability to *detect* mines/UXO
- The *quantity* of mines/UXO present within a given area

The authors further translate these three identified key components into a remarkably simple yet effective graphical representation. Figure 2.1, adopted and greatly simplified from the McAslan and Feigenbaum article, graphically depicts the cumulative anti-personnel mine threat from an area in Bosnia-Herzegovina.

As illustrated in Figure 2.1, *detectability*, ranging from most detectable in the bottom left to least detectable (and therefore more dangerous) at the top left, is plotted along the vertical axis. Conversely, *severity of harm*, ranging from the least amount of harm on the bottom left to the most amount of harm on the bottom right, is plotted along the horizontal axis. Finally, *quantity* is represented by the size of the plotted circle that is associated with a particular landmine type.

One can learn a great deal from studying the constructed graph. For example, a PMA-3 landmine is a small, low-metal content blast mine that is difficult to detect, but has a lower potential to cause harm primarily because of a fairly small primary charge (admittedly this harm scale is relative).

Conversely, the more ubiquitous PMR-2 landmine has a much greater severity-of-harm index but is fairly easy to detect. The PMR-2 essentially looks like

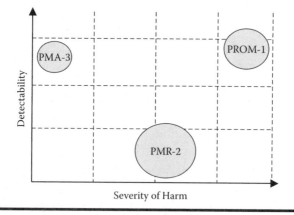

Figure 2.1   A graphical representation of a threat-based model relating to landmine removal as adapted and greatly simplified from McAslan and Feigenbaum (2000). In this example, threat is a function of landmine detectability, severity of harm, and quantity (indicated by circle size).

a grenade placed on top of a stick and stuck into the ground. The high harm severity rating is primarily due to the nature of fragmentation landmines in general. Fragmentation mines are normally more lethal because of associated shrapnel-related injuries.

Finally, the PROM-1, a Serbian bounding fragmentation mine, is both deadly and difficult to detect. Bounding fragmentation mines literally bound (that is, leap) some 3 feet into the air, exploding into an often powerful blast and resultant spray of deadly shrapnel.

As illustrated in Figure 2.1, in general, landmines located toward the top right of the graph represent a greater threat than those found toward the bottom left. Accordingly, the graph clearly depicts the types of landmines that represent the greatest threat to humanitarian deminers. It also represents a three-component threat model that is easily depicted in a two-dimensional format via increasing or decreasing the size of plotted landmine circles.

Unlike the previous logistics and baseball examples, where a more mathematical formula representation is used, here we see the use of a graphical representation. Yet both representations depict a surprisingly simple logic that effectively captures the essence of what truly drives a particular outcome in a succinct and easily understandable manner.

The Power of Good Logic

In the preceding pages numerous examples of outcome-related performance factors have been described. Let us quickly review these identified Y outcomes and associated x factors:

Life expectancy:
  – Infant mortality
  – Adolescent mortality
  – Maternal mortality
Human Development Index:
  – A long and healthy life
  – Knowledge
  – A decent standard of living
Container shipping:
  – Time cargo-filled vessel under way
  – Time in port
America's Cup sailing:
  – Tactics
  – Boat speed

    – Boat handling
Logistics productivity:
    – Number of aircraft required
    – Mission load per sortie
    – Sorties per aircraft per day
Baseball runs:
    – On-base percentage
    – Slugging average
ERW threat:
    – Munition type and related severity of harm
    – Detectability
    – Quantity

Note that the essence of each outcome, be it life expectancy, logistics productivity, baseball runs, or the threat posed by ERW, is captured by only a few critical performance factors—factors that clearly possess real oomph.

As such, the real power in creating a $Y = f(x)$ performance model is not simply the developed algebraic or graphical expression. Rather, it is the fundamental logic underlying the developed model. Fortunately, when we expend the effort to create this performance-related logic, it forces us to answer a basic but often overlooked question: What specific factors drive a particular performance outcome?

In many instances, we may be living under false and associated costly assumptions about supposed critical performance drivers—assumptions that may drive bad decisions and unwanted outcomes. It is suggested, then, that every organization needs not only its standard vision and mission statements, but also, perhaps even more importantly, a concise and succinct *performance statement* that clearly identifies those key factors affecting both wanted and unwanted performance outcomes. In short, a statement that contains those few but oh-so-critical oomph factors.

Creating Task Models

Before closing, it might be worth briefly mentioning one additional benefit in creating a performance model. Once critical performance variables or so-called *x* factors are correctly identified, they can often be further translated into critical tasks or work elements. The idea here is that a constructed performance model can drive a required work model (or task model).

This translation from performance to work model is especially well illustrated in some of the literature associated with emergency response efforts to natural or man-made disasters. Cuny (1999), for example, argues that the essential priorities in the initial phase of any emergency famine response operation are those that successfully address the major killers of malnutrition, measles, and diarrhea. In our performance-based framework, malnutrition, measles, and diarrhea are negative, unwanted x factors.

To successfully counter such unwanted factors, critical operational activities must include supplying food, immunizing people, and controlling diarrhea through the provision of clean water, sanitation, hygiene, and oral rehydration. Cuny notes that these identified tasks form the basic foundation of an initial famine response doctrine. Each of these critically identified tasks in turn requires a distinct set of operational activities and supporting resources. Yet such required resources and subactivities are always driven by an immediate need for food, immunization, and diarrhea control.

Fiedrich and others (2000) take a similar "critical few" approach when describing response needs to an earthquake. According to the authors, three response activities are especially critical when responding to an earthquake:

■ Search and rescue (SAR) work to remove people trapped in collapsed buildings
■ Stabilizing work to prevent secondary disasters (for example, dam failures, fires, and so on)
■ Immediate rehabilitation of transportation lifelines to improve the accessibility of so-called relevant areas, including hospitals, SAR areas, and secondary disaster areas

Note in this particular example that the immediate operational focus is primarily on SAR and SAR-related activities. However, as identified, another important focus area is purposely avoiding additional unwanted consequences associated with potential secondary disaster areas.

According to the authors, the main influencing factor for optimizing resource allocation in any disaster response is *time* (an especially critical x factor). This observation is especially true for time-constrained SAR activities in earthquake disaster response efforts. The reason for this imposed temporal constraint is available survival time for victims trapped in collapsed buildings.

For such victims, the probability of survival steadily decreases with time. This critical time-induced factor is further compounded by various other factors, including the starting physical condition of trapped victims, environmental conditions (especially temperature), and types of incurred injuries. The maximum survival time for victims trapped in a fallen building is usually 4 to 7 days.

The authors further identify a set of key operational tasks that they refer to as basic work elements during this critical 4- to 7-day response period. They further link required resources to each identified basic work element. Such basic work elements and associated resources include rescue (requiring SAR personnel), lift (requiring cranes and hydraulic extractors), load (requiring hydraulic excavators and wheeled loaders), transport (requiring trucks), spread (requiring dozers), and compact (requiring spreaders).

By adopting a performance-based modeling approach in regards to earthquake response, the authors have precisely and succinctly identified:

- Specific operational *tasks* that must be performed (e.g., rescue, lift, load, etc.)
- Within an established *timeframe* (in this case, 4 to 7 days)
- Using specific *resources* (e.g., dozers, trucks, cranes, and so on)
- In identified *areas* of operation (e.g., SAR areas, hospitals, and so on)

Note that in these latter two disaster response–related examples, you see only a handful of critical tasks driving the developed task models. In turn, each *task* model is driven by and linked to a critical few *performance* model. It is suggested that, all too often, we fail to correctly and adequately identify these critical few elements that add so much oomph to any attempted performance-related endeavor.

Summary

Performance represents an outcome, result, or accomplishment. A performance outcome is often expressed as a function of some set of critical variables or performance drivers. Although numerous variables can potentially affect a performance outcome, the real key is identifying those critical few variables that truly drive performance, and in understanding the interrelationships between and among such identified drivers. The important thing in better understanding performance is identifying the underlying logic or DNA of performance, a derived logic that succinctly and concisely describes what is true.

Chapter 3

S-Curves and
Performance Limits

A big part of my journey in better understanding performance has involved plotting literally thousands of individual performance records, ranging from sports events to global public healthcare to offshore oil production. What I have discovered in this plotting frenzy is that, irrespective of venue, industry, or business, there is a fundamental and repeatable set of concepts (you might even call them natural laws) that govern how gains in performance accrue and do not accrue over time.

Performance Improves Exponentionally

What I have learned is that performance improves in a roughly modified exponential or logistic-based functional manner. Here is an example:

A 50th percentile male at birth measures some 20 inches in length (the almost exact length at birth of our first grandson, Caden). In the first year of life, he adds another 10 inches to his height. In the second year, he adds another 4.5 inches, ending his first 2 years of life measuring about 34.5 inches in length. The third year results in 3.5 inches of additional growth, and the fourth year about 3.0 inches of growth. The fifth year adds an additional couple of inches. So at age five, our 50th percentile male is about 43 inches tall.

Over the next 10 years, he grows roughly between 2.0 and 2.5 inches per year except in his fourteenth year, when he experiences a short growth spurt of some 3.0 inches. Thus, on his fifteenth birthday, he now stands about 67 inches tall.

In his sixteenth year, he adds another 1.5 inches. In his seventeenth year, he adds an additional half inch. After that, there is not much growth at all. On his eighteenth birthday, he is 69.5 inches tall, or a bit shy of 5 feet 10 inches. Some 7 years later, on his twenty-fifth birthday, he still stands a bit shy of 5 feet 10 inches.

If you plot this growth rate through time, as graphically depicted in Figure 3.1, you observe that cumulative growth rises steeply in the first couple of years, not quite as steeply over the next 12 to 13 years, and then slows markedly, ultimately stalling out at about 18 years of age. After that, the curve is essentially flat.

Life cycle performance gains almost universally follow the same growth pattern as illustrated in Figure 3.1 for our 50th percentile male: growth, and then no growth. After getting off to a slow start, performance gains normally accelerate rapidly. This rapid acceleration results in a positive exponential increase that produces an initial steep and inflationary growth form. The length and magnitude of that inflationary growth period can vary widely, depending on the actual system of interest as illustrated in various examples throughout this and subsequent chapters.

Given enough time, however, limiting factors are encountered, and cumulative growth rates slow markedly. This slowdown results in a negative exponent increase, when performance accrual rates asymptotically approach some upper defined limit or capacity threshold (more about this toward the end of this chapter). This stalling-out phenomenon is almost universally observed in mature growth systems.

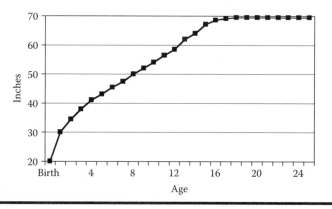

Figure 3.1 A graphical depiction of growth as a function of age for a 50th percentile male. Note the transitions from rapid growth to slowed growth to no growth, an almost universally exhibited life cycle growth pattern.

For our 50th percentile male friend, this stalling-out phase started at about 16 years of age and was completed about 2 years later. The resultant growth form, which resembles a somewhat modified looking S-shaped curve, is called a *logistic function*. Many processes follow this rather predictable, growth-related, S-shaped life cycle. This life cycle is, if given enough time, ultimately comprised of five distinct stages: birth, growth, maturity, decline, and finally death. The concept of a life cycle, originally used by biologists, is now routinely applied by historians, business people, psychologists, and epidemiologists, to name just a few. These folks use the life cycle concept to predict everything from the growth rate of epidemics, products, and companies to that of whole countries. Irrespective of specific application, however, all life cycles represent growth rate as a function of time. Such growth rate, however, is always zero before the beginning, and becomes zero again at the end.

As we move along a complete life cycle by passing through the successive stages of birth, growth, maturity, decline, and death, we find that if we plot the number or *frequency* of units at each individual life cycle stage, we usually get a bell-shaped frequency curve (that is, a normal curve). Conversely, the cumulative number of units of such plots, when continuously aggregated, form the shape of an S. S-shaped curves thus represent a visual and almost universal symbol for *cumulative* life cycle growth.

Normal Curves

Before exploring in some detail the development of S-shaped cumulative life cycle curves, it might prove valuable to spend just a bit of time first discussing the more familiar bell-shaped or normal curve. Remember, a bell-shaped or normal frequency curve and an S-shaped cumulative curve are just two different ways of displaying essentially the same data.

Figure 3.2 depicts an idealized bell-shaped curve or normal frequency distribution. In such an idealized depiction, all three measures of central tendency—mean, median, and mode—coincide. The *mean* represents an average. It is calculated by adding all values in a string of numbers, and then dividing by the number of cases or numbers (1 + 2 + 3 = 6 ÷ 3 = a mean of 2). The *median* is the halfway point in a group of numbers. And the *mode* is the most common value in that group or spread of numbers.

In a perfectly symmetrical distribution, as illustrated in Figure 3.2, all three measures of central tendency coincide. This is because the center point of the graph is simultaneously the most common value (that is, the mode), the halfway point with equal numbers of cases on either side (that is, the median), and the average or mean.

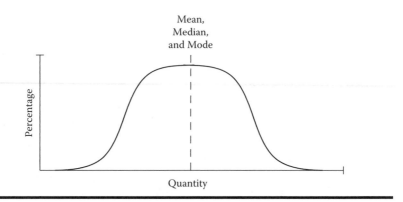

Figure 3.2   An idealized and perfectly symmetrical bell-shaped curve or normal frequency distribution. In such perfectly symmetrical normal distributions, all measures of central tendency (mean, median, and mode) coincide in the middle.

In real life, however, such curves are a bit skewed to one side or the other. In a skewed distribution, the "tails" look decidedly different (that is, they are not equal and instead appear asymmetrical). Figure 3.3 depicts left- and right-skewed frequency distributions, respectively. Note that the two tails no longer look exactly the same, as they did in Figure 3.2.

In such asymmetrical or skewed distributions, measures of central tendency no longer coincide with the exact same central point as they did in the perfectly symmetrical example illustrated in Figure 3.2. Rather (and as depicted in Figure 3.4), in a right-skewed distribution, the median or halfway point lies to the right of the mode (the most common value). In turn, the mean or average lies to the right of both the median and the mode.

In their book *Baseball Between the Numbers* by the Baseball Prospectus Team of Experts, the authors depict an interesting chart plotting *equivalent average* (EqA) for all players who played in Major League Baseball and affiliated leagues in 2004. EqA is somewhat akin to an expanded batting average metric. The metric is intended to do two things: (1) measure the offensive performance of a baseball player, and (2) make the result easy to understand. EqA combines a player's ability to hit for average, hit for power, draw walks, get hit by pitches, and steal bases. It also adjusts for the offensive level of the league and the hitter friendliness of differing ball parks. In short, EqA allows fans to compare apples to apples, or in this case, one player's offensive performance to another player's offensive performance.

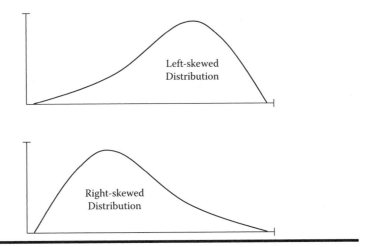

Figure 3.3 Left- and right-skewed distributions are depicted in the top and bottom graphs, respectively.

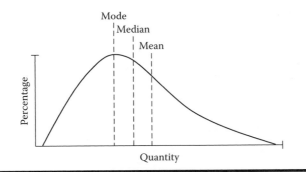

Figure 3.4 In right- and left-skewed distributions, measures of central tendency do not coincide exactly. As illustrated here for a right-skewed distribution, the median lies to the right of the mode, and the mean lies to the right of both measures.

The depicted EqA chart in *Baseball Between the Numbers* shows the following:

■ Minor League players have an EqA of less than .230.
■ Major League fringe players have an EqA between .230 and .260.
■ Major League regular players have an EqA between .260 and .300.
■ All-Star players have an EqA between .300 and .330.
■ Hall of Fame players have an EqA above .330.

As you might expect, the depicted frequency distribution is decidedly skewed to the right, with far fewer players comprising the right-hand All Star and Hall of Fame tail as compared to the opposing and much larger Minor League tail. Often, in such graphical depictions, the smaller tail of a right- or left-skewed distribution represents some type of performance limit or physical wall.

S-Shaped Curves and Logistic Functions

With my bell-shaped-curve diversion complete, let us now turn our attention to the even more interesting S-shaped cumulative curve. For introductory purposes, I will describe two examples, one fictitious and the other factual. First, the fictitious one.

After carefully considering different career options, you finally decide to go into the yacht brokerage business. The first 3 years, however, are extremely tough, and you do not sell any yachts. In year 4, you finally get a break and make your first big sale. The next year things are a bit better, and you sell two yachts. The following year, you sell three, and so on, with each successive year adding one additional sale.

This growth rate sustains itself until the thirteenth year, when you max out by selling ten yachts. The next year it is ten again. Then the following year you sell only nine, then eight, then seven, until the twenty-third year, when you are able to sell only one yacht. Over the next 3 years, you do not make any further sales. Facing certain career death, you decide to get out of the yacht-selling business altogether after being in the business for some 26 years.

Table 3.1 lists both your yearly and cumulative sales figures. Figure 3.5(a) plots yearly sales figures in a normal bar graph fashion, whereas Figure 3.5(b) plots cumulative sales via a line graph. You should instantly observe two things. First, note how perfectly symmetrical yearly sales distribution appears in Figure 3.5(a). This is the classical bell-shaped curve that we discussed in the preceding section.

But more importantly, note the appearance of Figure 3.5(b). It looks like a perfect S-shaped curve, doesn't it? That is when we plot cumulative frequency by adding previous year sales figures to the present year, and then plot that figure for each year; we get a graph form that looks like an S. But does this perfect S-shaped curve in this admittedly perfect fictitious example repeat itself in real life? The answer is an often surprising, but slightly skewed, yes!

In 1925, diesel locomotives started replacing steam locomotives within the U.S. railway system. At first, the replacement or exchange effort was fairly minimal. Then it began to pick up steam (or more accurately, diesel). Some 40 years later, there were almost 30,000 diesel locomotives moving freight and passengers along the nation's railroad system.

Table 3.1   Individual and Cumulative Per Year Yacht Sales

Year	Sales	Cumulative Sales
1	0	0
2	0	0
3	0	0
4	1	1
5	2	3
6	3	6
7	4	10
8	5	15
9	6	21
10	7	28
11	8	36
12	9	45
13	10	55
14	10	65
15	9	74
16	8	82
17	7	89
18	6	95
19	5	100
20	4	104
21	3	107
22	2	109
23	1	110
24	0	110
25	0	110
26	0	110

If you plot the cumulative frequency of this diesel locomotive-related growth, what does it look like? You guessed it. As illustrated in Figure 3.6, it looks like an S-shaped curve, although admittedly a bit of a stretched out S. Although in the real world, plotted S's are rarely perfectly formed because of related skewness, they nevertheless often have a characteristic S-shape look to them. This characteristic S-shape that we so often observe appears to be following some underlying law that is controlling both growth rate and resultant growth form.

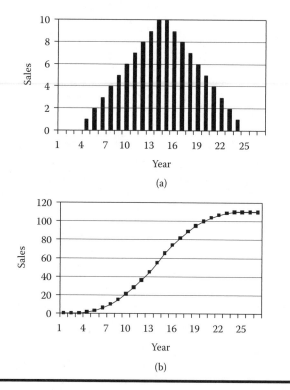

Figure 3.5   Graphical plots of frequency and cumulative frequency data from the idealized data table presented in Table 3.1. A frequency plot of the data results in a bell-shaped or normal distribution as illustrated in Figure 3.5(a). Conversely, a cumulative frequency plot of the same data results in an S-shaped curve form as depicted in Figure 3.5(b).

Mathematicians tell us that the underlying law describing this natural growth form is expressed mathematically as a *growth function.* Admittedly for anyone somewhat mathematically impaired, such equations can be a bit overwhelming to decipher. Fortunately for our discussions here, it is important to note only that the simplest mathematical function that produces the common S-curve is called a *logistic function*, a phenomenon first described in the literature by mathematician Pierce Verhulst in 1845.

A logistic function is derived from a law that states that "the rate of growth is proportional to both the amount of growth already accomplished and the amount of growth remaining to be accomplished." Why the S looks like an S is controlled by the fact that if either one of these quantities is small, the rate of

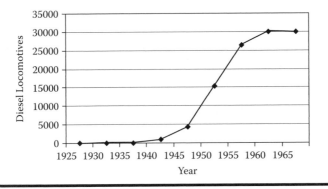

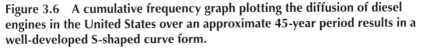

Figure 3.6   A cumulative frequency graph plotting the diffusion of diesel engines in the United States over an approximate 45-year period results in a well-developed S-shaped curve form.

growth itself will be small. That is why the top and bottom of the S are flat; they represent little to any growth.

Conversely, the rate of growth is greatest in the middle, thereby giving the S both height and shape. In the middle, growth accomplished and growth remaining are both sizable. Furthermore, the idea that growth remaining to be accomplished implies that, at least theoretically, a finite growth limit or capacity exists—a so-called performance wall. This supposed barrier to continued growth is assumed to stay constant throughout the entire growth process. However, as described in Chapter 4, we will discover how such system-imposed growth ceilings can sometimes get a bit of a lift via innovation.

The logistic function is a remarkably simple yet fundamental law relating to growth. The law is founded upon the underlying principle that natural growth must ultimately obey certain limiting factors, factors that produce this commonly observed growth ceiling (or asymptote) and the associated S-shaped curve.

In this and the following chapters, I will use this brief explanation of S-curves and logistic functions to examine an array of performance gains from diverse settings. Irrespective of setting, however, each example follows the same characteristic growth pattern, albeit at highly varying magnitudes. After getting off to an initial slow start, a steep and often prolonged relative rise in performance gain occurs, followed ultimately by a pronounced slowdown in growth. Such resultant slowdowns, typically characterized by ever smaller gains in performance over correspondingly longer time intervals, create the characteristic S-shaped curve as depicted in Figures 3.5(b) and 3.6.

Here's another example. Referring to the discussion in Chapter 1 of the relationship between healthcare spending and life expectancy, Figure 3.7 plots coun-

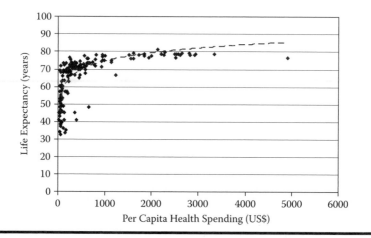

Figure 3.7   A plot of life expectancy in years as a function of per capita healthcare spending normalized to U.S. dollars (using 2006 data) by individual country. Note, as illustrated, a point is reached rather early where continued increases in healthcare spending do not correspond to continued increases in life expectancy, irrespective of amount spent.

try-specific per capita healthcare spending normalized to U.S. dollars against life expectancy plotted in years. As illustrated in Figure 3.7, going from essentially not spending anything on healthcare to spending about $300 per person per year makes a substantial difference in life expectancy on an individual country basis—a difference that means successfully extending life expectancy on average from some 35 years to 75 years.

Conversely and also as illustrated in Figure 3.7, going from spending $300 to $2,000 or even to $5,000 per person makes little, if any, difference in life expectancy. Indeed, the highest growth rate in life expectancy occurs between spending $0 and about $200 per person per year for healthcare.

Note that the shape of the generated curve in Figure 3.7 rises steeply to a certain life expectancy limit, and then flattens abruptly. Once this upper limit (or asymptote) is reached, additional spending, regardless of amount or associated effort expended, has little or no effect in extending years of life. Once again, growth ultimately ends in no growth.

As already noted, this same growth form is universally seen in other performance domains as well. Figure 3.8 depicts world record progression in the women's 400-meter hurdles track event. Note that for ease of illustration and graph form comparison, time is translated into miles per hour in Figure 3.8.

Notice a fairly steep initial improvement, followed by a flattening or stalling-out effect. In this latter slowdown phase, incremental improvements in speed are

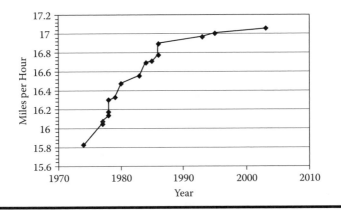

Figure 3.8 World speed record progression in the women's 400-meter hurdles track event. Observe how, relatively speaking, fairly steep initial gains in speed are followed by a flattening effect beginning in about 1985.

smaller and occur over increasingly longer time intervals. Some seventeen miles per hour seemingly approaches the human capacity threshold (or wall) for this particular track event. It is also important to note that, in this example, the overall increase in speed is relatively minor, less than 8 percent over an approximate 30-year period.

In contrast, Figure 3.9 depicts the world water speed record progression for propeller-driven speedboats with internal combustion engines. A steep initial rise in speed is observed, followed by a marked decrease in subsequent gains in speed. This observation is well supported by an overall increase in speed of approximately 150 mph in the first 50 years, as compared to an increase of only 50 mph over the next 50 years. The total increase in speed, however, which covers some 100 years, is an amazing 2,000 percent.

Finally, Figure 3.10 depicts a generic conventional oil discovery curve. The discovery curve plots the cumulative volume of discovered oil reserves (normally measured in barrels of oil) against some measured effort, often expressed as a function of time or number of exploratory wells drilled. Note that a steep initial discovery period accounts for the bulk of gains in cumulative volume. This steep initial inflationary period is subsequently followed by a significant slowdown in cumulative growth, characterized by the top flattened portion of the curve; this slowdown is often associated with major oil companies abandoning their exploration efforts and leaving the area to smaller, later arriving independents. As a result of this often observed exodus, such curves as illustrated in Figure 3.10 are called *creaming curves* in the oil industry, indicating where and when the cream of any exploration effort by volume begins and ends.

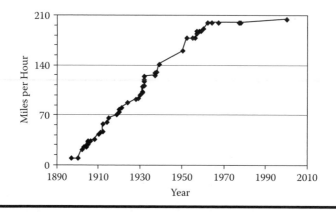

Figure 3.9 World water speed record progression for internal combustion engine, propeller-driven speedboats. As depicted, a steep initial rise in speed is followed by a marked decrease in subsequent speed gains, resulting in a flattening-out effect beginning in about 1955. Irrespective of magnitude, note the pronounced similarities between Figures 3.8 and 3.9.

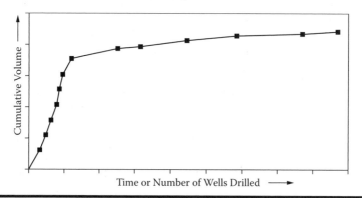

Figure 3.10 A hypothetical plot of cumulative oil volume as a function of time or number of wells drilled. Note how steep initial gains reach a pronounced asymptote with a resultant marked decrease in additional discoveries. Such curves are called creaming curves in the oil industry.

Thus, whether we are talking about human growth, human health, human speed, powerboat speed, cumulative oil discovery rates, or myriad other processes, there is a fundamental and repeatable set of concepts regarding how performance improves and grows over time. In such fundamental instances, rapidly accelerating initial performance gains eventually approach some upper capacity threshold (or bounding limit) and essentially begin to stall and flatten out. In essence, rapid growth is followed by slowed growth that, in turn, translates into no growth.

When performance gains do begin to stall and flatten out, doing more of the same, whether it involves spending more money on healthcare or drilling more wells, often results in little if any additional result. As illustrated in the case of the 50th percentile male as represented by my grandson Caden, he really cannot train for height after his eighteenth birthday, regardless of how much effort or time he might exert in doing so.

This observed performance-flattening phenomenon as a function of time represents an almost universal truth. If you observe, for example, how humans acquire a particular skill as a function of practice, the resultant plot looks almost exactly like all the previously depicted S-curve plots. At the beginning of the skill acquisition life cycle, you normally experience very rapid gains in improvement as a function of practice trials. Such rapid gains initially result in a very steep performance curve. With time, however, accrued gains decrease markedly, and the curve begins to flatten out. Eventually, and despite repeated practice trials, gains in improvement are minimal at best. Once again, observe the rapid growth, slowed growth, and essentially no growth performance life cycle model.

Does this supposed universal observation mean then that once you reach a performance asymptote there is essentially nothing that you can do to accrue additional gains? As discussed in Chapter 4, the answer is sometimes yes and, unfortunately, sometimes no. But first, let us discuss a bit more about the limits of performance.

The Limits of Performance

The S-shaped curve obeys a strict law, one founded on the principle that there is a finite growth ceiling, thus creating the top, flat portion of the S. But we may express this growth-related reality in another way. Irrespective of where a product or process is on an S-curve, there is a finite amount of growth remaining or available. Indeed, whether you are talking about the mechanical limits of speedboats or the biomechanical limits of human sprinters, there are always limits, given enough time.

The realities of such limits are both good and bad. In the case of wanting to continuously improve performance they can be, well, limiting. In the case of something like an unwanted epidemic, however, they can be a good thing. Let us briefly consider the effects of such limits on the overall growth pattern of an epidemic. But first, a bit of epidemiological background may prove helpful.

Epidemiology is the branch of medicine that deals with the incidence, distribution, and control of diseases and other factors relating to health. Modern mathematical epidemiology, our specific interest here, began with the introduction of what is known as the *SIR model*. The SIR model, formulated by two very bright mathematicians named William Kermack and A. G. McKendrick over 70 years ago, still forms the basic building blocks of most infectious disease models currently in use today.

The three letters in the SIR acronym are extremely important. They represent the three primary states that any member of a population can occupy with respect to a contagious disease.

- The S part of the SIR model stands for *susceptible*. This means that an individual in a population is vulnerable (or susceptible) to a certain disease, but has not yet been infected by it.
- Conversely, the I stands for *infectious*. This designation implies that the individual not only is infected with the disease but also can infect others.
- Finally, R stands for *removed*. Removed means that an individual has either recovered from the disease or has died from the disease. Either way, the person is no longer susceptible and is thus removed from the population of potential susceptibles.

According to the SIR model, new infections can occur only when an infected individual, commonly referred to as an *infective*, comes into contact with a *susceptible*. Without a susceptible being present, an infective has no one to infect.

When the two do come into contact, however, the susceptible can become infected. The chances of this happening depend on how infectious the disease is and the susceptibility and other characteristics of the susceptible.

According to the SIR model, when an epidemic does occur, it often follows a predictable path. For epidemiologists who study such epidemics, the path followed by an epidemic over time resembles logistic growth in the shape of an S-curve. Not surprised?

The rate at which new infections grow is also dependent on the size of both the infective and susceptible populations As illustrated in the bottom of Figure 3.11, when an infectious disease is in its early growth stages, the infected population is small and, correspondingly, so is the rate of new infections. At the beginning of an epidemic there simply are not enough infectives around to cause much harm, resulting in the S-curve being represented by only the bottom, fairly flat portion.

This initial slow-growth phase is also the most opportune time to control a spreading epidemic. Often, the removal of even a few infectives from a population can drive a disease back into remission. This is why at the start of an outbreak like bird flu, literally hundreds of thousands of chickens, ducks, and the like are destroyed. The intent is to remove infectives as rapidly as possible, thus preventing the deadly disease from spreading uncontrollably.

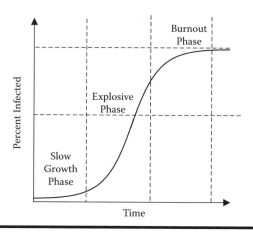

Figure 3.11   A graphical plot of the three life cycle phases of an epidemic and resultant S-shaped growth pattern.

If the number of infectives continues to grow, however, an epidemic typically enters the explosive phase of logistic growth. This middle (and certainly unwanted) phase is illustrated in the middle part of Figure 3.11.

Remember, a logistic function is derived from a law that states that "the rate of growth is proportional to both the amount of growth already accomplished and the amount of growth remaining to be accomplished." Why the S looks like an S is because if either one of these quantities is small, the rate of growth itself will be small. That is why the top and bottom of the S are flat.

Yet the law describing logistic growth also states that rates of growth are greatest in the middle. In this middle area, the growth accomplished and the growth remaining are both sizable, relatively speaking. Thus, in the case of epidemics, the reality that rates of growth are greatest in the middle means that there are plenty of infected and susceptible individuals available who can come into contact with each other. As a consequence of this infective and susceptible abundance, the rate at which new infections occur is maximized.

The explosive phase of an epidemic, graphically speaking, represents the steep part of the S-shaped curve (again, see the middle part of Figure 3.11). Unfortunately, most epidemics in the midst of such explosive growth are essentially impossible to stop—a scary proposition for us susceptible humans.

Eventually, however, even the most ravaging and out-of-control epidemics have their limits. Epidemics, like wildfires, will eventually burn themselves out if given nothing but enough time. Their eventual demise is due to the fact that because there are only so many people who can become infected, the supply of susceptible targets will eventually dry up. Epidemiologically speaking, this represents the final burnout phase of logistic growth and is graphically depicted in the top part of Figure 3.11.

So from an initial slow-growth phase to an explosive phase to a final burnout phase, the trajectory of an epidemic follows the characteristic S-shaped growth pattern. This growth pattern, in turn, can be explained by the logistic growth model.

Epidemics teach us that, given enough time, essentially any growth system will ultimately reach some bounding limit. That is, one can only grow or infect so much until one eventually hits some limiting wall. Performance systems, be they human or mechanical, are no different. (See the preceding example of the women's 400-meter hurdles track event, in which some 17 mph seemingly represents some finite human speed limit for this event.)

Such limiting examples imply that, at least theoretically speaking (and often realistically speaking as well), given enough time, potential performance improvement capacity is finite. Fortunately, in some instances, improvements continue to accrue over sustained time periods. One only has to look at continued increases in computing power, for example, to realize this observation. Yet eventually, any system will reach some bounding capacity limit—even computer processing speed!

Before illustrating the sometimes harsh realities of performance limits, ceilings, or walls, I define three applicable terms that are graphically illustrated in Figure 3.12: total performance capacity, realized performance capacity, and unrealized performance capacity.

■ *Total performance capacity* (TPC) is the maximum performance level a system can potentially attain. For our 50th percentile male example, TPC in height is a tad less than 70 inches. For a 1-gallon jug, TPC is 1 gallon. Although you might wish to pour more fluid into the jug, a 1-gallon jug is and always will be a 1-gallon jug. In many instances, however, TPC may

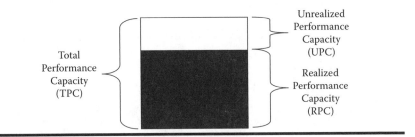

Figure 3.12   As illustrated, total performance capacity (TPC) is comprised of realized performance capacity (RPC) and unrealized performance capacity (UPC).

not be fully attained or realized due to a number of factors. For example, although human life expectancy is currently at a maximum of some 80 years, inadequate and grossly underfunded public healthcare systems, compounded by HIV/AIDS, prevent many countries from reaching even a 40- or 50-year average life expectancy rate. Sadly in such instances, TPC is not being fully attained.

■ *Realized performance capacity* (RPC) is the capacity that has already been attained or realized in any system. The 50th percentile male, for example, has already realized some 20 inches of those available 70 inches at birth.

■ *Unrealized performance capacity* (UPC) is the remaining capacity that has not been attained and is still unrealized. In our usage, UPC equates to the late Tom Gilbert's performance improvement potential (PIP) concept. It essentially represents what's available to ultimately work with from a performance improvement perspective, or what is still available between the limits of performance. Returning once again to our 50th percentile male, if TPC is some 70 inches and RPC at birth is 20 inches, UPC must be 50 inches (70 inches – 20 inches = 50 inches). This male certainly has the potential capacity over the next 18 years to grow an additional 50 inches, but not much more, due to the biologically imposed limits of TPC.

Per these simple definitions, you can create some equally simple mathematical representations:

TPC = RPC + UPC, or total performance capacity equals realized performance capacity plus unrealized performance capacity. If the 50th percentile male at birth is 20 inches long (the RPC), and you know that he will grow another 50 inches (the UPC), then TPC is 70 = 20 + 50, or 70 inches.

RPC = TPC – UPC, or realized performance capacity equals total performance capacity minus unrealized performance capacity (20 = 70 – 50).

UPC = TPC – RPC, or unrealized performance capacity equals total performance capacity minus realized performance capacity (50 = 70 – 20).

The amount of UPC (the amount of unrealized growth available in a system) can vary greatly, depending on both total growth capacity (represented by TPC) and the amount of growth (RPC) that has already taken place. As such, available UPC is often little more than a function of life cycle stage. Remember the epidemic analogy: at the beginning, there is (unfortunately) lots of available UPC, whereas at the end (thankfully), UPC is zero.

A good example at the low end of available UPC in a system is the overall increase in speed of thoroughbred racehorses, as illustrated in Figure 3.13. This figure plots speed record progression in the 1.25-mile Kentucky Derby, a race

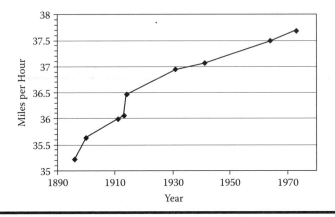

Figure 3.13 Record progression in speed for the 1.25-mile Kentucky Derby thoroughbred horse race.

that is held on the first Saturday of each May. As depicted, the first official speed record (note that times have once again been converted to miles per hour for simplicity) was set in 1896 at a speed of 35.23 mph. This first record consumed some portion of TPC and represents the initial RPC. Since that initial effort in 1896, eight subsequent speed records have been set in the Kentucky Derby.

The last record for the Derby was set in 1973 by a horse named Secretariat, who won the derby in a run equivalent to a speed of 37.69 mph. This latest record, however, represents an overall increase in speed of only some 7 percent over a 77-year period (1896 to 1973). Since 1973, only one horse has even come close to Secretariat's record, when in the 2001 Kentucky Derby, Monarchos ran the Derby in an average speed of 37.52 mph. Monarchos' run came up just shy of Secretariat's record by a mere 0.17 mph.

Since no real increase in speed has occurred since 1973, you could take a stab and estimate that the top speed in the Kentucky Derby might be some 38 mph. This 38 mph represents our defined TPC. Using this hypothetical but probably fairly realistic 38 mph TPC figure, Figure 3.14 plots changes in RPC and UPC as a function of time.

Note that the first record (#1) in Figure 3.14 consumed some 93 percent of total performance capacity. This means that if we are at least approximately right about our 38 mph TPC figure, then from the very beginning of the Kentucky Derby there was very little UPC available for additional accruals in speed.

Secretariat's record-setting run in 1973 consumed a bit over 99 percent of TPC, leaving possibly less than 1 percent of UPC available for subsequent improvements in speed. This observation may explain why more than 30 years later, no

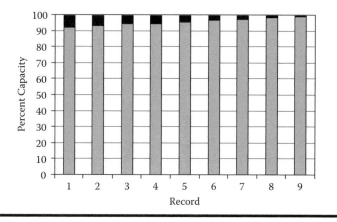

Figure 3.14 A plot of realized performance capacity (in gray) and unrealized performance capacity (in black) for the Kentucky Derby, based on a 38 mph total performance capacity figure.

horse has beaten Secretariat's Kentucky Derby record, despite the fact that over 1 million registered thoroughbred racehorses have been born since 1973.

Although you might wish to wager on a horse at the Kentucky Derby to win, place, or show, I caution you on betting that a horse will break Secretariat's record. Admittedly, such a record-breaking run is possible, but it probably represents a very low-probability bet at best.

The realities of these physical or biomechanical-induced limits in thoroughbred horse racing are perhaps best illustrated in Figure 3.15. The World Series of thoroughbred horse racing is the Triple Crown, a grueling schedule of three races in 5 weeks beginning with the just-described 1.25-mile Kentucky Derby on the first Saturday of May. Two weeks later, it is the 1.1875-mile Preakness, followed 3 weeks later by the significantly longer 1.5-mile Belmont Stakes. Since 1919 and as of this writing, only eleven horses have captured the coveted Triple Crown grand prize, including such greats as War Admiral, Citation, Secretariat, Seattle Slew, and the latest winner in 1978, Affirmed.

Figure 3.15 plots the distribution of winning times in 1-second increments for the Belmont Stakes, using data since 1926 when the race was fixed at its current 1.5-mile length. Note that the bulk of winning times cluster somewhere between 148 and 150 seconds. Also note that the lone left-tail score of 144 seconds belongs to our friend Secretariat.

By any standard, Secretariat was an exceptional racehorse. In fact, in early June 1973, a sort of equine and sports history was made when Secretariat appeared in the same week on the front covers of *TIME*, *Newsweek*, and *Sports Illustrated*. Standing at 16.2 hands and weighing some 1,200 pounds, the 3-year-

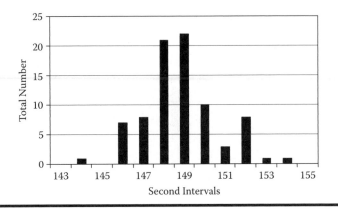

Figure 3.15   A frequency plot of winning times in seconds for the 1.5-mile Belmont Stakes thoroughbred horse race. Note the lone 144-second entry bounding the left tail representing Secretariat's phenomenal run in 1973.

old chestnut colt with three white feet set track records in both the Kentucky Derby (which we noted still stands) and the Preakness. But it was Secretariat's run in the Belmont Stakes on June 9, 1973, that clearly demonstrated his incredible prowess and speed. Track announcer Chic Anderson called during the race that "Secretariat is widening now, he is moving like a tremendous machine."

On that day, Secretariat not only set a new record (that, as illustrated in Figure 3.15, has never even been approached by another horse), but in so doing, he beat the second-place finisher by an incredible 31-length lead. Clearly, Secretariat's run in the Belmont Stakes may have hit the limits of equine performance. Indeed, one can only speculate whether we will ever witness another run like the one that took place during the Belmont Stakes in 1973.

We can also treat human speed progression in the men's 100-meter sprint track event in much the same way that we analyzed horse speed. As depicted in Figure 3.16, the first official record for the 100-meter men's sprint was set in 1912 at a speed of approximately 21.1 mph (once again I have converted time to miles per hour). The current record, set by Jamaica's Asafa Powell on September 9, 2007, in Rieti, Italy, is some 23.0 mph.

From 1912 then, overall speed in the men's 100-meter track event has increased by only about 9 percent. Since 1988, however, when Carl Lewis of the United States broke the record in Tokyo, Japan, times have decreased little (from 9.92 seconds to 9.74 seconds), despite records being set or tied ten times since Lewis's memorable run.

If you guess that 23.25 mph approximates TPC in the men's 100-meter sprint, then, as illustrated in Figure 3.17, the first record consumed about 91 percent of TPC, close to the same number of 93 percent in our thoroughbred

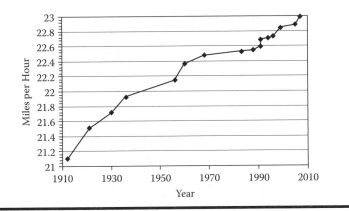

Figure 3.16   World record progression in speed for the men's 100-meter track event.

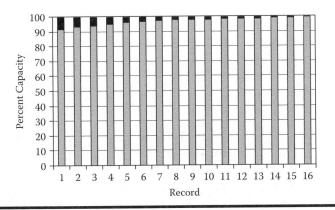

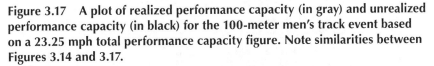

Figure 3.17   A plot of realized performance capacity (in gray) and unrealized performance capacity (in black) for the 100-meter men's track event based on a 23.25 mph total performance capacity figure. Note similarities between Figures 3.14 and 3.17.

racehorse example. Indeed, if you compare remaining UPC in both Figures 3.14 and 3.17, you see that human and thoroughbred sprinters appear surprisingly similar. As will be discussed in Chapter 4, such similarities may be due to the realities of evolution and where humans and horses are currently located in the evolutionary speed life cycle.

By contrast to such biomechanical speed limitations, let us briefly examine mechanical speed record progression. I will use world record speed progression for internal combustion engine, propeller-driven speedboats, which were first plotted in Figure 3.9. The first official world record was set in 1897 at a speed of 9.73 mph. The current record set in 2000 is an amazing 205.49 mph. As noted earlier, however, overall increases in speed over the past 50 years have only been some 50 mph. In fact, since 1962, speed has increased by only 5.075 mph. Accordingly, suppose you choose top speed (TPC) of 225 mph based on current and foreseeable engine and boat designs and fuel sources.

As depicted in Figure 3.18, the first record consumed or realized only about 4 percent of TPC. Compare this initial RPC figure to the two previous horse and human speed examples where initial RPC was in the low 90 percent range. In fact, for a number of years (as illustrated in Figure 3.18), there was ample UPC to continuously increase the speed of internal combustion engine–propelled water craft—a speed potential reality that was increasingly realized over time.

Unrealized performance capacity can vary greatly depending on type of system and associated realized performance capacity. It seems that in some performance systems, especially biologically based ones, available UPC is often quite limited. Such limitations are well illustrated in Figures 3.14 and 3.17. Additionally, biological systems are by their very nature often highly resistant to marked improvements in performance. This harsh reality is primarily caused by a prolonged evolutionary period that may be currently approaching some theoretical biomechanical limit or threshold.

In other instances, however, such as often found in much younger and newer technologically based systems, there is often (but by no means always)

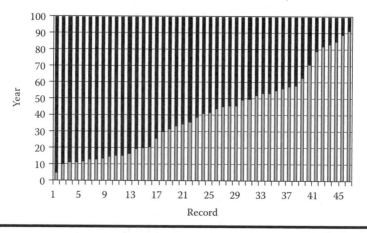

Figure 3.18   A plot of realized performance capacity (in gray) and unrealized performance capacity (in black) for world water speed record progression for internal combustion engine-powered speedboats based on a 225 mph total performance capacity figure. Note the marked difference in available unrealized performance capacity between this plot and Figures 3.14 and 3.17.

ample performance improvement potential. In such systems, as illustrated by speed progression in race boats, improvement efforts can often be sustained over extended periods of time, albeit at usually decreasing magnitudes over increasingly longer time intervals.

Projecting Unrealized Performance Capacity

Before leaving this discussion of performance limits and exploring the sometimes positive role of innovation, I would be somewhat remiss if I did not consider at least briefly how you might actually go about assessing total performance capacity and unrealized performance capacity in a system.

The ugly truth is that assessing TPC and UPC is sometimes difficult if not downright impossible. This observation is particularly true in earlier growth phases, especially if you lack good historical data upon which to make subsequent growth predictions.

Consider, for example, Figure 3.19. The figure plots cumulative natural gas production as a function of time from a presently producing gas field in western Wyoming. Note that field production as illustrated by the graph is currently in a relatively early and inflationary growth phase period. What is your best guess regarding TPC as represented by ultimate total gas production? At this early stage in logistic growth, it is difficult to ascertain, especially if you have little historical basis upon which to make a prediction. Figure 3.19 illustrates the

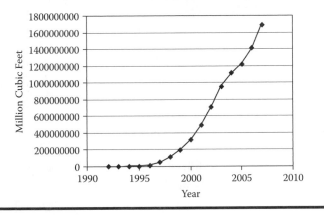

Figure 3.19   A cumulative production plot from a natural gas field in western Wyoming. Note in this example that the field is in an early, inflationary growth phase resulting in a poorly developed S-shaped cumulative growth form.

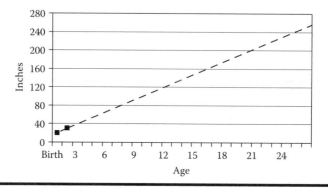

Figure 3.20   A projected 25-year growth plot for Fred based on only 1 year's worth of growth data.

problem and harsh reality of projecting TPC and remaining UPC in the early stages of logistic growth.

Let us examine another example in somewhat greater detail that we are more familiar with, the 50th percentile male friend whom I will finally name: Fred.

Let us begin by assuming that we have absolutely no idea how tall Fred will grow from birth to his twenty-fifth birthday, although we need to make some type of estimate. Additionally, let us also assume that we do not know anything about logistic growth and S-shaped curves. All we do know is that at birth Fred is 20 inches tall. A year later, on his first birthday, we measure Fred again and find that he is now exactly 30 inches tall.

Not knowing what else to do and with absolutely no other available data, we create a graph like the one in Figure 3.20 that spans a 25-year growth period. Next we plot Fred's height at birth, which is 20 inches, and then his height at 1 year of age, which is 30 inches. This we do know. Finally, we take out little more than an old-fashioned straight edge and connect the dots, plotting a dashed straight line to extrapolate his height at 25 years. This admittedly crude technique gives us an approximate projected height of 21 feet 9 inches on Fred's twenty-fifth birthday, so at this point, you can estimate that Fred will grow to a height of nearly 22 feet by the time he reaches 25 years of age.

If you wait until Fred's fifth birthday, however, and apply the same technique, the new calculation now indicates an approximate 7.5-foot height on Fred's twenty-fifth birthday—a significant reduction from our earlier almost 22-foot height projection. The result of this 5-year projection effort is shown in Figure 3.21.

You can again repeat the process on his tenth birthday, as illustrated in Figure 3.22. The new 10-year calculation still projects that Fred will grow to about

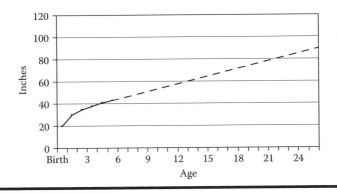

Figure 3.21   A projected 25-year growth plot for Fred based on 5 years of growth data. Compare to Figure 3.20.

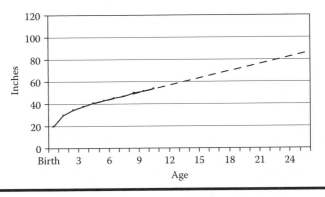

Figure 3.22   A projected 25-year growth plot for Fred based on 10 years of growth data. Compare to Figures 3.20 and 3.21.

7.5 feet by the time he reaches his twenty-fifth birthday. With two similar projections over a 5-year basis, a height of 7.5 feet now seems fairly probable.

If you again repeat the same process on Fred's fifteenth birthday, this time (as depicted in Figure 3.23), you come up with the same projected 7 feet 6 inches height figure as you did on his tenth birthday. With now three essentially similar measured height projections over a ten-year period, you can feel increasingly confident—in fact almost assured—that Fred will be about 7.5 feet tall on his twenty-fifth birthday.

Five years later, on his twentieth birthday, you repeat the same projected calculation technique (see Figure 3.24). This time, however, you notice that over the last few years, Fred's growth rate has been essentially zero. Not being sure how to extrapolate this new data, you simply project the top and flat part of the

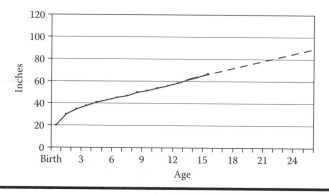

Figure 3.23 A projected 25-year growth plot for Fred based on 15 years of growth data. Compare to Figures 3.20–3.22.

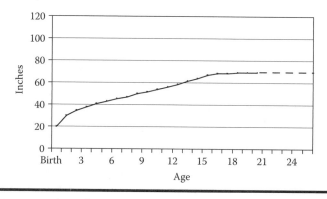

Figure 3.24 A projected 25-year growth plot for Fred based on 20 years of growth data. Note the now observed and marked flattening effect in growth at about age 17. Also see Figures 3.20–3.23.

curve. Accordingly, you now project that Fred will attain a height of only some 5 feet 10 inches on his twenty-fifth birthday.

Finally the big day comes, and Fred actually turns 25. No more extrapolation and projection, you simply take out the old measuring stick and accurately measure the guy. As shown in Figure 3.25, your twentieth birthday projection of approximately 5 feet 10 inches turns out to be fairly accurate after all.

Note how, over the 25-year period, as you periodically projected Fred's height you were forced to change your numbers based on new and ever-changing data. The approximate 22-foot height became a 7 feet 6 inches figure that finally changed to the actual 5 feet 10 inches figure. Only when the growth curve

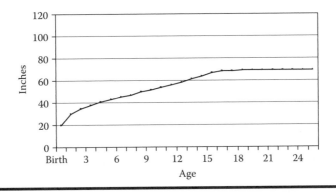

Figure 3.25   An actual 25-year growth plot of Fred. Note differences in projected height as a function of time, as illustrated in Figures 3.20–3.25.

began to flatten out were you able to project a final height with any real accuracy. Admittedly, however, as time progressed, each subsequent projection got you closer to the actual and final 5 feet 10 inches truth.

As illustrated by Fred, such growth or performance accrual projections are often fraught with danger. This observation is particularly true when you are projecting logistic growth in an early and inflationary growth phase with poor or nonexistent historical data. Every now and then in the business world, you hear about a projection that goes terribly awry, often at a significant loss to the projecting company and affected financial stakeholders. One reason for such inaccurate estimates may be that those companies are dealing with a logistic growth pattern that has no historical data from which to gauge or base ultimate growth rates.

When projecting anticipated performance gains, you must be extremely careful. Knowing now that such gains normally follow a logistic growth pattern, this acquired understanding should give you pause and a conservatism in making performance-related growth predictions. As illustrated in the numerous examples presented in this chapter, what goes up must ultimately flatten out. That is, there are ultimate limits to almost everything.

Yet does this observation mean that there is absolutely no way beyond these supposed performance-imposed limits? The answer, as you will discover in Chapter 4, is that it depends. It depends primarily on the potential for growth to begin anew via the process of innovation. Or in biological speak, for clado-genesis to beget renewed anagenesis.

Summary

Irrespective of venue, industry, or business, there is a fundamental law regarding how performance improves over time. A law that is best captured under the concept of logistic growth that states: the rate of growth is proportional to both the amount of growth already accomplished and the amount of growth remaining to be accomplished. Accordingly, after sometimes getting off to a slow start, rapidly accelerating or inflationary performance gains eventually approach some limiting threshold or wall. Subsequent improvement efforts, regardless of effort or cost expended, often result in little additional result.

The fact that there are such limits means that every performance system has a certain total performance capacity (TPC) that controls ultimate growth or gain. Based on life cycle position and theoretical capacity thresholds, unrealized performance capacity (UPC) can thus vary widely. Accordingly, in some instances, performance improvement potential is quite limited. In other instances, however, significant improvement potential may exist. Better understanding the amount of improvement potential available in any given system can not only better guide related performance improvement efforts, but also assist in setting more realistic improvement expectations. However, calculating TPC and available UPC may be more difficult than imagined, especially in the early stages of logistic-based growth, compounded by the poor availability of historical data.

Chapter 4

How Innovation (Sometimes) Begets Improvement

As described in Chapter 3, performance improves in a rather predictable fashion irrespective of venue, industry, business, and just about anything else. Initial slow growth often gives way to rapid growth, only to be eventually replaced once again by slow growth that ultimately ends in no growth. This slow growth, fast growth, slow growth, no growth cycle results in a characteristic S-shaped curve that represents a very visual and almost universal symbol for cumulative life cycle growth. The slowdowns in performance, characterized by ever-smaller gains over correspondingly longer time intervals, create a terrace, step-like, or flat-top appearance in growth form.

Overlapping S-Curves and What They Mean

Yet there are exceptions to this flat-top look. I found that some performance curves contain multiple step- or terrace-like features. That is, they represent composite curves consisting of one S-shaped curve stacked upon another.

A good example of this observed stacking phenomenon is illustrated in Figure 4.1. The graph depicts world land speed record progression, plotted in miles per hour. As illustrated, it appears that two S-shaped curves are present, one overlying the other at about the 400 mph asymptote. Initially I was not able to account for the observed shape illustrated in Figure 4.1.

After a bit of research, I found that each S-shaped portion of the curve represents a unique and decidedly different technological lineage. A lower internal combustion engine, wheel-driven technology is replaced by a faster jet engine, thrust-based technology. As illustrated in Figure 4.1, this switchover occurred in the early 1960s.

Note that the wheel-driven lineage mimics fairly closely the formula for relatively steep initial gains, followed by a pronounced slowdown and an eventual flattening out. Also observe that the introduction of a new technology, in this case a jet engine–powered vehicle, did not result in a drastic and instant jump in performance. Rather, the introduction of the new technology served more as a performance catalyst, jump-starting the performance improvement process anew as illustrated by renewed incremental gains in vehicle speed.

As I became increasingly aware of this innovation-induced, multiple S-curve phenomenon, I started seeing more examples. Admittedly, sometimes such examples were extremely subtle. Figure 4.2 plots progression in the men's high-jump track-and-field event. On close examination, you can faintly observe four distinct terraces or steps composing the overall shape of the graph. Once again, after a bit of research, I discovered that each observed terrace correlates perfectly with a distinctive high-jumping technique.

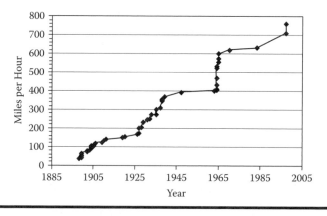

Figure 4.1 World land speed record progression. Note graphical plot includes both a lower internal combustion engine with wheel-driven technology and an upper and faster jet engine, thrust-based technology. As depicted by the 400 mph asymptote, this switchover from a wheel-driven to a thrust-based technology occurred in the early 1960s.

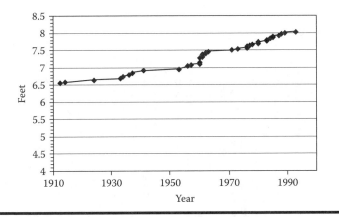

Figure 4.2 World record progression in the men's high-jump track-and-field event. Note the plot of four faint terraces that perfectly coincide with differing high-jumping techniques.

Figure 4.3 depicts actual gains in height associated with each new jumping technique. As illustrated in Figure 4.3, over time the scissors kick gave way to the western roll, which was replaced by the straddle jump that, in turn, was replaced by the Fosbury flop. From the data plotted in both Figures 4.2 and 4.3, one can observe, for example, that the straddle jump added more inches than the western roll.

Yet as previously observed, each new jumping technique did not result in an instant and spectacular gain in height. Rather, the introduction of each new technique seemed to serve more as a catalyst for renewed incremental gains in performance. And that may be the real role of innovation: innovation begets or renews incremental performance improvement.

As a side note to Figure 4.3, it is interesting to observe that no new record in the high-jump event has been set since 1993, when Cuban Javier Sotomayor cleared 8.04 feet. This lack of continued improvement since 1993 suggests that it may be time for the introduction of yet another new innovation in high-jumping technique. An alternative explanation for the lack of continued progress (as discussed in Chapter 3), however, may be the simple fact that Javier's jump finally reached the biomechanical limits for this event.

About Innovation

Before continuing our discussion of the role of innovation in enhancing performance, it may prove beneficial to first provide a bit of a review about

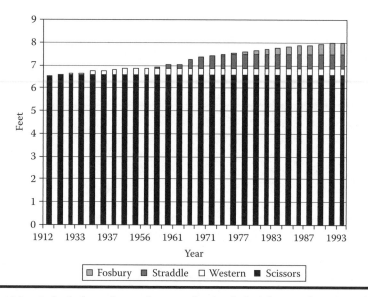

Figure 4.3   A depiction of actual accrued gains in height as a function of high-jumping technique.

innovation, including introducing an innovation classification system. As you will learn, different innovation types are often associated with different performance improvement processes. Accordingly, some innovations represent a catalyst for renewed improvement, whereas others seem to serve as the actual improvement workhorses.

Innovation is defined as the successful exploitation of new ideas. Hargadon, in his insightful book on innovation entitled *How Breakthroughs Happen: The Surprising Truth About How Companies Innovate*, describes innovation as the process of linking people, ideas, and objects in new and novel ways. This connotation of newness that is so often associated with innovation, however, needs a bit of clarification. Innovations certainly represent something new and novel. Yet they also represent something old.

George Basalla captures this old-new relationship quite well in his scholarly book entitled *The Evolution of Technology*. According to Basalla, technology represents the "made" world. An artifact is the fundamental unit of study in this world. And continuity prevails throughout the made world.

The existence of continuity in the made world is important. It implies that novel artifacts can arise only from antecedent artifacts. In other words, novel artifacts are always linked in some way to previous artifacts. New artifacts, therefore, never represent pure or original creations of theory, ingenuity, or fancy. Rather, they represent a modification or elaboration of something previous; innovations always exploit the past in some new and unique way. They represent both a break from and a tie to the past. More specifically, innovations are always built from pieces of the past.

Humans, for example, probably first picked up a rock and used it to pound something. We then chipped away at the rock in order to make a better pounding device. Next, we probably tied a stick to our chipped rock for better leverage. The rock morphed into a metal head, and the stick became a handle. Thus, we have what we now call a hammer. From rock and stick to metal head and handle, one can trace or link the pieces of the past (the rock and stick) to the present and new hammer.

Not all innovations like the hammer, however, are successfully adopted by a society. Basalla notes that the number of inventions available for adoption in a society has always been greater than the number of inventions actually adopted. Accordingly, how innovations are adopted and diffused throughout a society is in and of itself a fascinating and important topic. Fortunately for us, the late Everett Rogers spent much of his professional career studying innovation diffusion. Indeed, the name Everett Rogers and the study of the diffusion of innovations are virtually synonymous.

In his fifth edition book entitled *Diffusion of Innovations*, Rogers' defined diffusion as the process in which "an innovation is communicated through certain channels over time among the members of a social system." According to Rogers, the adoption of an innovation over time allows us to plot a diffusion curve in much the same way that we plotted performance curves in the previous chapter.

Perhaps no longer surprising, the adoption of an innovation usually follows a normal bell-shaped curve when plotted over time on a frequency basis. And even less surprising, if the cumulative number of adopters is plotted, the result is (as you probably already guessed) the classic S-shaped curve form. Always remember that a bell-shaped frequency curve and an S-shaped cumulative frequency curve are just two different ways to display essentially the same data.

Figure 3.6 in the previous chapter plotted the diffusion of diesel locomotives in the United States through time. As illustrated in the cumulative-based frequency plot (and following Rogers' innovation-related adoption hypothesis), an S-shaped curve is formed. Indeed, you can clearly see in the plotted data how initial slow adoption gave way to rapid adoption that is followed once again by slowed adoption, as the integration of diesel locomotives eventually reached a limiting plateau.

Rogers defined an innovation *adopter* as someone who has made a conscious decision or choice to make full use of an innovation as the best course of action available. The rate of adoption in such instances is the relative speed with which an innovation is adopted by members of a social system. Rogers further defined different types of adopters, depending primarily on when they do their adopting. He named these various adopters in temporal order as *innovators, early adopters, early majority, late majority,* and *laggards.*

Rogers further described how adopter distribution results in an S-curve that initially begins to rise slowly. This initial slow rise is due to the fact that, in the beginning, there are only a few adopters who will make a decision to use the new innovation. With the passage of time, however, the curve accelerates rapidly to a maximum, representing a point where about half of the individuals in the system have adopted the innovation. The curve then proceeds to increase over time at a gradually slower rate, as fewer and fewer remaining individuals adopt the innovation. Eventually, a point is reached when there are no longer any adopters left in the system to adopt, and the top of the S-curve is finally reached.

Once again we see an almost complete life cycle and corresponding S-shaped curve form. In this instance, the S-shaped curve consists of four distinct stages represented by slow initial adoption, rapid adoption, slowed adoption, and finally no adoption.

Rogers made an interesting observation when he noted that the part of the S-shaped diffusion curve that represents a roughly 10 to 20 percent adoption rate is the very heart of the diffusion process. After that critical point is reached, the diffusion of a new innovation more or less takes on an almost unstoppable life of its own. Think back to the S-curve plot of an epidemic in Chapter 3. Remember that once an epidemic enters an explosive phase, it is almost impossible to stop until it eventually peters out.

Accordingly, in the beginning of an innovation cycle, we want to do everything possible to *start* it. Conversely, in the beginning of an epidemic cycle we want to do everything possible to *stop* it. In both systems, however, once we get past this initial birth phase and into the next succeeding explosive phase, there is very little that we can often do to actually change course trajectory. The good news is that, from a business perspective, once an innovation is successfully launched, we do not have to spend as much money on advertising because a truly successful innovation will more or less sell itself.

Rogers correctly cautioned us, however, to remember that diffusion S-curves are innovation and system specific. That is, they describe only cases of *successful* diffusion where an innovation spreads to almost all of the potential adopters in a social system.

In reality, many innovations are not successful, and therefore do not produce the characteristic S-shaped curve. For example, although thousands of consumer products appear on store shelves and in media advertisements each year, most actually fail to become success stories. In such instances and without Rogers' critical identified 10 to 20 percent achieved adoption rate, the diffusion curve looks more like an inverted and short-lived V as opposed to a more graceful, sustainable, and profitable S.

Just as all innovations are not equally successful, nor are all innovations equally innovative. This differing innovativeness topic is addressed in the following section.

Innovation Types

If you begin this discussion of differing types of innovations by thinking about an innovation as representing only a technological object or artifact (admittedly, innovations can also represent new processes, methods, techniques, and so on), you can think of that object, be it a car, washing machine, or computer, as constructed of individually distinct components. *Components* thus represent one definable dimension of any technological object. K. B. Clark, in a paper written on technological evolution that was published in 1985 in the journal *Research Policy*, defined a component as "a physically distinct portion of a product that embodies a core design concept."

Some innovations, therefore, involve only the fundamental change of internal components. A good example is the introduction of the digital camera. In this component-related innovation example, the form of the camera has not changed dramatically: film cameras and digital cameras look similar. However, the internal components and associated core design concepts of a digital camera are fundamentally different when compared to a film camera. Consumer buying habits are also changing as a result of this component-driven innovation.

Any technological object, irrespective of type or function, also has a distinct shape or look. We call this look-related dimension a technology's *form*. Many innovations simply involve changing an object's form. A classic example of a form-related innovation is Japan's introduction of small cars in the 1970s. As a result of this change in car form, consumer car-buying habits also significantly changed.

Henderson and Clark, in an article featured in *Administrative Science Quarterly* in 1990, named such innovations in form "architectural innovations." Going from a mono-hulled sailboat to a multi-hulled sailboat is another good example of an architectural innovation or change in form.

The type and physical characteristics of components, along with linkages between and among those components, determine form. In some instances, very minor changes in components may result in substantial changes in form. Additionally, form and its associated characteristics and linkages of internal components determine functional capability. Functional capability in turn affects actual performance outcomes.

Similar to the work of Henderson and Clark, Harold Blackman and I published an article in 2006 in the journal *Performance Improvement*, using these same dimensions of form and components. We further combined these two dimensions with associated changes in magnitude to construct a simple 2 × 2 matrix for classifying innovation types. To further simplify our classification system, we elected to number innovative categories using the designators Types I, II, III, and IV.

This admittedly simple numerical-based classification system is different from those of previous authors, who use more descriptive terms in their respective innovation classification systems. Our proffered system, however, attempts to develop a more generic innovation classification system as opposed to the more manufacturing- or consumer-specific categories developed by previous authors.

The resultant innovation matrix is illustrated in Figure 4.4. The depicted matrix in Figure 4.4 should be viewed, however, more as a continuum than as a discrete set of fixed bins. We certainly admit that there is a great deal of gray matter among and between our four defined quadrants. Accordingly, there can be more or less change within any given innovation type.

Type I Innovations

As illustrated in Figure 4.4, Type I innovations represent only very minor changes in both form and internal components. Many authors call Type I innovations incremental innovations. A Type I innovation is analogous to the more commonly used term *improvement*. Although any single Type I innovation usually has only an incremental improvement effect, given enough time, the accumulation of such innovations can represent rather substantial overall improvements

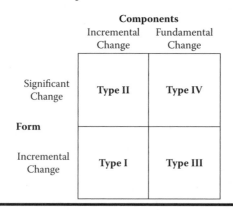

Figure 4.4 A developed innovation taxonomy based on the attributes of changes in form and components.

to an existing technology or system. Accordingly, Type I innovations often represent the real workhorse when it comes to performance improvement.

In the product-related business world, Type I innovations mainly improve the competencies of established firms. They do little, however, to enhance the position of outside players trying to penetrate an established market. This reality is primarily due to the fact that Type I innovations have only a minor effect on consumer buying habits.

Type II Innovations

As depicted in Figure 4.4, Type II innovations represent significant changes in form but only very incremental changes in internal components. Japan's strategy to make smaller cars in the 1970s represents an excellent example of a series of Type II innovations.

Type II innovations can vary widely in the magnitude of a change in form. The recent introduction—or more correctly, reintroduction—of front-loading washer and dryer sets is an example of a fairly low-order Type II innovation change. Yet surprisingly, relatively subtle changes in form can have disproportionate effects on consumer buying habits. Such effects, in turn, can adversely affect established firms in a given market. The introduction of small cars by the Japanese in the 1970s greatly eroded the then-dominant position of American automobile manufacturers, a dominant position that has to this day never fully recovered.

Type III Innovations

Type III innovations represent fundamental changes in internal components, but only minor changes in form. Transitions from analog to digital television or from mechanical to digital watches are two examples of Type III innovations. Henderson and Clark called Type III innovations modular innovations.

Type III innovations require a corresponding fundamental change in core concepts and knowledge. Although film and digital single-lens reflex cameras look very similar (that is, both have essentially the same form), they have fundamentally different internal components. Additionally, they also require fundamentally different types of science and engineering to develop and manufacture: film science and film engineering are fundamentally different than digital science and digital engineering.

Type III innovations have the very real potential to dramatically redefine an existing market. They also represent significant threats to established firms. Traditional film manufacturers, for example, are greatly threatened in this new digital camera world of ours. Indeed, given enough time, large, traditional film manufacturers will likely perish altogether.

Type IV Innovations

Type IV innovations, commonly termed radical innovations in the literature, represent significant changes in form as well as fundamental changes in internal components. The introduction of the steam engine, automobile, television, and personal computer are classic examples of Type IV innovations.

Type IV innovations often create whole new markets. They can also negatively affect, if not outright eliminate, existing markets. The horse-and-buggy market, for example, never recovered after we adopted automobiles as our primary means of transportation. Nor did the record and tape markets after the digitization of music.

If one could somehow measure the degree of innovative change, Type III and IV innovations clearly represent more dramatic or innovative innovations. Yet, as stated, Type II innovations often have a disproportionate effect on consumer buying habits.

As I will examine in the following section, the relationship between innovation type and associated gains in performance is a bit more complicated. As I will argue, it is actually Type I innovations that serve as the real workhorse for accruing continuous yet incremental gains in performance. Type I innovations often form the real backbone of observed inflationary performance growth.

Innovation and Performance Gains

Figure 4.5 plots increases in water depth over time for offshore exploration rigs drilling for oil in the Gulf of Mexico. Note that starting at a water depth of a bit less than 20 feet in the 1940s, today's offshore rigs have the ability to drill in water depths of some 10,000 feet, an incredible accomplishment.

This ever-increasing deep-water accomplishment depicted in Figure 4.5 is a function of continuous innovation. From barges to fixed platforms to jack-ups to semi-submersibles to drillships, the oil industry is constantly innovating and improving. Yet the oil industry is not solely interested in simply being able to drill in ever-greater water depths. Rather, it is interested in finding and profitably producing oil. Accordingly, we must ask how Figure 4.5 translates into actual gains in performance as measured by the amount of produced oil.

Figure 4.6 plots the resultant outcomes of Figure 4.5 as expressed in thousands of barrels of oil produced daily in the Gulf of Mexico. Note that Figure 4.6 depicts production from both shallow- and deep-water oil fields. Here

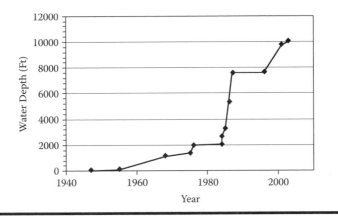

Figure 4.5 Increases in water depth over time for offshore exploration rigs drilling for oil in the Gulf of Mexico. Note that Figure 4.5 represents improvements in the means for producing oil in the Gulf of Mexico area.

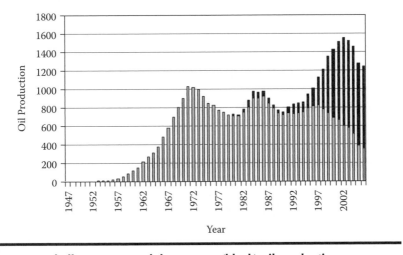

Figure 4.6 Shallow- (gray) and deep-water (black) oil production measured in thousands of barrels of oil produced daily from the Gulf of Mexico. Whereas Figure 4.5 represents the means, Figure 4.6 represents the outcome or end results of that means.

we define the difference between shallow and deep water at about the 1,000-foot mark. This 1,000-foot water depth typically separates shallow- and deep-water offshore drilling technologies, a depth that necessitates the transition from fixed (or legged) drilling platforms to deeper-water floating semi-submersible and ship-based drilling technologies.

As illustrated in Figure 4.6, average annual oil production in the Gulf of Mexico from shallow-water oil fields is in a mature and declining growth stage. Conversely, deep-water oil production is in an early and inflationary growth phase. This latter early-growth phase is a direct result of gains acquired via the varying processes of innovation.

In performance speak, Figure 4.5 represents the *means*, whereas Figure 4.6 depicts the *ends*. Although the means represents an interesting technology-related topic all by itself, our interest here is in the interrelationship between the means and the ends—in being able to quantify the empirical relationship between advances in technology and actual accruals in performance.

The evolution of the world water speed record (as introduced in Chapter 3) serves as a good starting point in illustrating a common pattern between innovation type and resultant gains in performance. Upon closer examination, we find that the history of the world water speed record is actually comprised of three distinct innovation shifts, represented in Figure 4.7 as three distinct technological lineages. The identified lineages represent different types of engines used for propulsion:

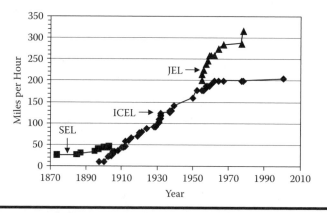

Figure 4.7 Differing lineages associated with world water speed record progression, including an earlier steam engine, propeller-driven lineage (SEL), a middle internal combustion engine, propeller-driven lineage (ICEL), and a later jet engine, nonpropeller-driven lineage (JEL).

- An early steam engine, propeller-driven lineage
- A middle internal combustion engine, propeller-driven lineage
- A late jet engine, nonpropeller-driven lineage

As illustrated in Figure 4.7, the first official world water speed record was set in 1874 at a speed of 24.61 mph. Power for this initial record-setting run was provided by a steam engine. The steam engine is considered by many the single most important Type IV innovation of the entire industrial revolution. Some credit Thomas Newcomen with inventing the first practical steam engine. Newcomen's invention was initially used in 1712 to power water pumps in the tin mines of Cornwall and in the coal mines of northern England. Many others, however, give the real credit for the development, practical use, and associated diffusion of steam engine technology to James Watt.

Irrespective of who deserves such initial credit—both gentlemen accomplished a great deal—the steam engine transformed the mining and manufacturing industry. It also transformed the transportation industry, initially enabling widespread railroad transport and later leading to the creation of the first steamboat. Interestingly, it turns out that the most innovative part of creating a steamboat did not involve the engine, fuel, boiler, or hull. Rather, it involved the propelling mechanism that physically linked the steam engine and the water.

As depicted in Figure 4.7, gains in speed incrementally improved through time within the steam engine technology lineage via a series of Type I innovations, as represented by incremental advances in speed. Such innovations and associated incremental increases in speed culminated in a final speed record of 45.06 mph set in 1903. This final steam engine–produced record represents an improvement in speed of some 83 percent over a relatively short 29-year period.

In 1897, an internal combustion engine powered a speedboat that set the first world water speed record for this new technology lineage. The introduction of the internal combustion engine, a Type III innovation, represents a fundamental change in an internal component (that is, the type of engine used).

Somewhat surprisingly, however, the addition of this new lineage resulted in a net decrease in speed of some 29 mph, going from the then steam engine–powered record of 39.1 mph to an initial internal combustion engine speed record of only 9.73 mph. One can only imagine the jeers and associated condemnation this new innovative technology must have received when it was first introduced.

It was not until 1911, some 14 years later, that the internal combustion engine was able to propel a boat faster than a steam engine–propelled boat. With the addition of time and the continued accrual of incremental Type I innovations, however, the internal combustion engine technology lineage eventually increased the speed of water craft from its modest 9.73 mph beginnings to the current 205.5 mph record. This amazing increase in speed represents a within-lineage performance improvement of some 2,000 percent over a 107-year period. Obviously, humble beginnings can turn into staggering performance success stories if given enough time and sustained Type I innovation-related efforts.

But this latter statement should not be interpreted as meaning that the increase in performance for the internal combustion engine–based lineage represents a smooth, linear progression over time. Rather, speed accruals have proceeded in fits and starts. As illustrated again in Figure 4.7, from 1900 to 1950, the internal combustion engine lineage increased in speed from 9.73 mph to 160.32 mph. This represents a performance improvement in speed of some 1,500 percent over roughly the first 50 years. Also note that this performance accomplishment was achieved primarily by the continuing accrual of frequent, yet relatively low-magnitude Type I incremental innovations accruing one small increment at a time.

Over the next 50 years, from 1950 to 2000, speed records increased from 160.32 mph to the current 205.5 mph record, representing only a 28 percent gain in performance. In fact, from 1962 to the present, a within-lineage gain of only 5 mph is observed. This stagnation of performance gains within the internal combustion engine technology lineage is caused by a marked decrease in both the frequency and magnitude of incremental gains associated with Type I innovations. It appears that the unrealized performance capacity of the internal combustion engine lineage was exploited by the early 1960s.

The final innovation to date in pursuit of the world water speed record is the addition of the jet engine technology lineage, representing yet another Type III innovation. The first record for this lineage was set in 1955 at 202.32 mph. This initial record represents an increase in speed of 23.83 mph over the then world water speed record of 178.49 mph. This latter speed record was set in the internal combustion engine technology lineage in 1952. Currently, the world water speed record is 317.6 mph, recorded in 1978 by Australian Ken Warby while driving the jet-powered *Spirit of America* speedboat.

My research to date (with the warmly acknowledged help of two very good friends) indicates that Figure 4.7 represents a fairly common pattern between technological innovation and performance. This relationship, when plotted, looks like a series of individual S-shaped curves, each one stacked upon the other.

In this discovered innovation-related generic pattern, the introduction of a new innovation creates a new technological lineage, representing an initial innovation shift. The start of such a new lineage or shift, however, is rarely immediately associated with significant gains in performance, and thus represents only the beginning or initial lower flat portion of a newly emerging S-shaped curve.

This commonly observed phenomenon of a lack of immediate significant gains in performance is well illustrated in Figure 4.8. Figure 4.8 depicts world record speed progression in sailing across the Atlantic Ocean in a west-to-east direction (that is, the fastest sailing direction across the Atlantic). As illustrated in Figure 4.8, the first record was set by the mono-hull *Atlantic*, skippered by Charlie Barr in 1905. It took Barr and his crew 12 days, 4 hours, 1 minute, and 9 seconds to make the transatlantic crossing. This recorded crossing time translates into an average speed of some 10 mph.

Barr's record stood for an incredible 75 years before finally being topped by skipper Eric Tabarly and his crew in 1980 in the multi-hulled *Paul Ricard*. Note that going from a single- to a multi-hulled sailing vessel represents a rather significant Type II innovation in form. This resultant Type II innovation increased overall average sailing speed, however, by a bit less than 2 mph, going from an average speed of 10.02 mph to a speed of 11.94 mph.

As depicted in Figure 4.8, the real dramatic increases in speed came from within the multi-hull technology lineage, especially among the faster catamarans. The latest record plotted in Figure 4.8 was set by American skipper Steve Fossett and his crew in 2001. They made the west-to-east transatlantic passage aboard their 38-meter catamaran *PlayStation* in an amazing 4 days, 17 hours, 28 minutes, and 6 seconds, a time that translates into an overall average speed of 25.78 mph. From the initial record set by the mono-hull *Atlantic* to Fosset's innovative catamaran *PlayStation*, overall speed has increased some 150 percent over a 96-year period.

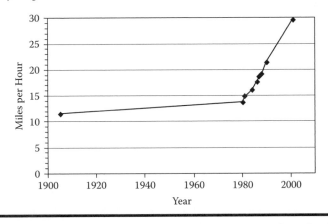

Figure 4.8   World sailing speed record progression across the Atlantic Ocean in a west-to-east direction. Note the lack of speed progression until 1980 when multi-hulled racing sailboats were first introduced.

Additionally, Fossett went on to repeat this remarkable speed feat in the even more challenging Jules Verne Trophy, an around-the-world, nonstop crewed sailboat race. Sailing in the same boat but now renamed *Cheyenne*, Fossett and his crew accomplished the journey in a staggering and exhausting 58 days, 9 hours, 32 minutes, and 45 seconds, averaging 18.37 mph. This incredible speed feat shattered the previous record of 64 days, 8 hours, 37 minutes, and 24 seconds (a 14.08 mph average speed) set by the French in 2002 in a catamaran named *Orange*.

Performance gains primarily accrue through a series of incremental Type I innovations within a particular technology lineage. Such innovations commonly have a fairly high initial frequency after the start of a new lineage, often exhibiting a positive exponent increase with compound growth (the steep part of the S-curve). Within this Type I innovation-dominated high-frequency phase, however, individual performance gains generally remain relatively small. Yet in some instances, and as illustrated by the extraordinary records set by Fossett and his crews, fairly substantial within-lineage performance gains sometimes occur as well.

Given enough time, however, Type I innovations almost always eventually stagnate and begin to stall out. Such slowing in incremental improvement frequency and resultant gains leads to a performance curve that begins to flatten abruptly, representing a now negative exponent increase and the initial formation of the top of the S. In this more mature phase, few performance gains accrue, and the lineage becomes more or less stagnant, at least from a performance growth perspective.

In such mature growth situations, performance gains seem to be able to begin anew only through the introduction of a new innovation and the resultant creation of a new technology lineage. The start of this new lineage in turn leads to a new round of incremental Type I innovations, which in turn accrue continued gains in performance. Accordingly, Type II, III, or IV innovations seem to beget Type I innovations. Type I innovations, in turn, result in incremental gains in performance (at least for awhile).

This described innovation life cycle applies equally well to many other innovation-dependent endeavors. Writer Avery Johnson, for example, in a December 11, 2007, *Wall Street Journal* article on the pharmaceutical industry notes that many of the industry's major blockbusters, like Pfizer's $80 billion cholesterol-fighting Lipitor drug, are nearing the end of their extremely lucrative patent life. Equally disturbing is the fact that currently there are not many equally lucrative, patent-protected replacements coming out of the drug-making pipeline. Indeed, many inside and outside of the industry observe that as of late, Big Pharma seems to be on a bit of a losing streak.

Johnson does an excellent job describing this late-mature, innovation life cycle pharmaceutical industry state when he notes that as a "byproduct of the late-19th-century chemical business, pharmaceutical research thrived for more than a century by finding chemical combinations to treat diseases. But after contributing substantially both to human health and drug industry profits, it has failed to produce significant innovations in recent years." Just as significant gains in speed failed to accrue in the latter years of internal combustion engine–powered race boat development, the same slowdown phenomenon seems to be presently affecting the pharmaceutical industry.

Unfortunately, spending more is not always the answer either. According to Johnson, despite the fact that the pharmaceutical industry is "spending tens of billions of dollars on research and development, pharmaceutical companies have fewer and fewer drugs to show for it." Johnson observes that in 2006, the industry received approval from the Food and Drug Administration for just eighteen new chemical-based drugs. This number compared to fifty-three new drugs receiving approval in 1996, only ten years earlier. What is even more disturbing is that many of the eighteen 2006-approved drugs are simply chemical variations of already existing prescriptions.

In the article, Robert Massie, president of the American Chemical Society's database of chemistry research, provides an extremely insightful observation when he compares such drug-based chemical research to the introduction of metal drivers in golf. Massie calls the initial introduction of metal drivers a huge innovation success, but now it is just incremental at best. According to Massie, the golf industry is currently just "coming out with drivers that are a little longer or rounder." The same supposedly holds true for chemical-based research: drugs being developed today are just a bit longer and rounder!

Yet, potentially, there is some good news as the pharmaceutical industry launches a new, biotechnology-based drug lineage based to a great extent on recent advances in genetic research. This new biotech-based lineage will rely predominantly on biologists producing proteins from live cells as opposed to previous practices of chemists making pills out of elements from the periodic table. To date, however, the promise of such biotech-based drug development has been somewhat disappointing. One can only hope that similar to the equally slow start of the internal combustion engine speedboat lineage, with time subsequent accruals in biotech-based drug development will turn into incredible medical success stories for increasingly prescription-dependent and aging human populations.

In some cases, however, the addition of a new lineage does not lead to successive incremental gains in performance. For example, when the aluminum pole replaced the bamboo pole in pole vaulting (a track-and-field event), this classic Type III innovation led to few successive gains in performance. In fact, cumulative gains, as illustrated in Figure 4.9, amounted to only a fraction of an inch for the entire aluminum pole vault lineage.

Conversely, the addition of the next-technology lineage, that of the fiberglass pole (representing another Type III innovation), did result in a series of renewed, albeit incremental gains in pole vaulting performance. As my colleague Harold Blackman mused, perhaps these observed performance differences are due to the specific nature of the lineages themselves—that is, the element aluminum may leave little room for improvement. Conversely, a material such as fiberglass has several dimensions with which changes may result in incremental improvements in performance. This possibility is clearly illustrated in the fiberglass-associated lineage graphically depicted in Figure 4.9, as compared to the aluminum lineage.

Finally, many who study the formation of technology lineages and their successive within-lineage improvement or evolution often see a comparative model or analog in the biological world. This biological-related topic is briefly explored in the following section before I make some final general observations about the role of innovation and corresponding gains in performance.

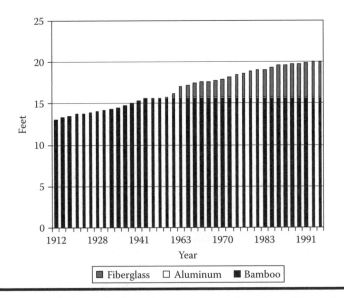

Figure 4.9 Cumulative gains in pole vaulting as a function of type of pole used. Note that only very minor gains in height resulted with the use of aluminum poles, whereas significant gains accrued via the later introduction of poles comprised of fiberglass.

Biological and Technological Evolution

Many who study so-called advancements in technology have discerned that some of the principles of evolutionary biology are quite similar to the observed principles of evolutionary technology. Yet although such comparisons between the biological and technological worlds are compelling, especially for tool makers, they may, in fact, be more coincidental than real.

Evolutionary biologists like to speak of *lineage*, a lineal descent from a common source. Think of a branch on a tree. The branch represents a lineage. It descends from the tree's trunk.

Anagenesis describes a single lineage undergoing incremental change. The tree branch grows or evolves slowly over time. Type I innovations, representing incremental gains in performance, are analogous to the biological concept of anagenesis. Given enough time, however, the branch stops growing. This is a common anagenic characteristic: growth, then no growth. This no-growth state represents the inevitability of biology. It may also possibly represent the inevitability of a single technology lineage as well. Yet it is important to note that although a lineage may stop growing, this does not necessarily imply that it stops performing or functioning. Although our tree branch may be in a mature, almost no-growth stage, it is still very much alive and performing its function in a biological sense.

Cladogenesis is the division or split of a single lineage into another lineage. Cladogenesis is likened to the start of a new tree branch. It is also analogous to Type II, III, and IV innovations. Cladogenesis begets something new. Once cladogenesis occurs, anagenesis may begin anew. Cladogenesis is thus the catalyst that restarts anagenesis. These various evolutionary biological concepts are illustrated in Figure 4.10.

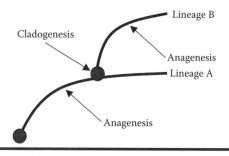

Figure 4.10   A graphical depiction of the biological-related concepts of anagenesis and cladogenesis. As depicted, cladogenesis often begets renewed anagenesis.

In a biologically analogous way, performance gains accrue primarily via anagenesis or Type I innovations. Or more specifically, performance gains accrue incrementally within a single innovation lineage. Although there are certainly exceptions to this incremental nature of performance gains, huge performance gains are, in reality, the exception rather than the norm. Accordingly, performance improvement is primarily an anagenic process via Type I innovation.

Eventually, however, anagenesis begins to stagnate. As a result of this stagnation, the tree branch eventually stops growing, but as noted, certainly does not stop performing. Lineage A in Figure 4.10 graphically illustrates this anagenic reality. So do the thoroughbred and human speed graphs depicted in Chapter 3.

A way to restart this anagenic-imposed reality is to add a new lineage. This new condition is accomplished via cladogenesis, or via Type II, III, or IV innovations. Once a new lineage forms, anagenesis begins anew. Given that cladogenesis begets anagenesis, innovation begets performance improvement. Type II, III, or IV innovations represent the catalysts that can potentially restart improvement anew via Type I incremental innovation.

The Role of Innovation Shifts

In the Harbour and Blackman article entitled "Innovation—The Other 'I' Word Associated with Performance," my co-author and I proffered a few generalizations that may be worth repeating here. Admittedly, such generalizations are always fraught with danger, because notable exceptions do occur and they are real. Yet based on all of my frenetic plotting activity described here and in Chapter 3, I think I can offer at least some tentative observations regarding the interrelationship between innovation and performance.

Major, radical innovation shifts occur periodically through time. Although such shifts do occur, they seem to take place much less frequently than we assume or portend. Major innovation shifts from a technological view are mostly associated with Type III and IV innovations, and to a lesser degree with Type II innovations.

There is little evidence that the introduction of a Type II, III, or IV cladogenic innovation is immediately accompanied by significant gains in performance. Indeed, in many instances, the initial introduction of such innovations actually results in a loss in performance, no gain in performance, or at best, only a very minor accrual in measurable performance.

Actual performance gains within a technological lineage appear to occur primarily through the continuous accrual of incremental Type I anagenic innovations. It appears that from an actual performance improvement perspective, Type II, III, and IV innovations serve mainly as a catalyst that permit a renewed round of associated Type I innovations to occur with resulting incremental gains in performance (that is, cladogenesis begets anagenesis). In some cases, however, such innovations are not followed by Type I incremental gains in performance. Although the introduction of Type II, III, or IV innovations potentially provides the basis for a new round of Type I–related performance gains, they by no means guarantee it. In such instances, cladogenesis does not beget renewed anagenesis.

Given enough time within a particular technological lineage, Type I innovations and associated accruals in performance begin to stagnate, with performance growth markedly decreasing in both frequency and magnitude, and unrealized performance capacity approaching zero. Unless a new technological lineage is established via a Type II, III, or IV innovation, performance capacity is essentially capped. Such capping phenomena are especially observed in biologically based systems that are in a very mature state of their evolutionary growth cycle.

These derived and admittedly initial findings may nevertheless have broad significance and practical application to the general field of performance improvement. In the early 1990s, for example, business process reengineering (BPR) was hailed by many, including Hammer and Champy in their widely selling business book *Reengineering the Corporation—A Manifesto for Business Revolution*. As the title implies, the two authors championed BPR as a radical new manifesto for business revolution, one they boasted would be capable of generating quantum, 1,000 percent leaps in performance. Unfortunately, these promised gains in performance did not materialize, and companies quickly became disillusioned with the whole BPR concept. (Such disillusionment, I might add, was much to the consternation and economic loss of a contingent of highly paid BPR consultants.)

Reflecting a bit on the whole BPR debacle, it may be that changes generated from earlier BPR efforts were possibly akin to Type II, III, or even IV innovations. Consequently, they may have served only as catalysts that, through time, actually did result in significant process-related gains, although probably not to the degree initially promised. Instead, these potentially more modest derived gains would most likely have accrued via incremental (and certainly for many, by not very astonishing) gains in performance.

If this observation is correct, the whole performance improvement community, including its technological innovator counterparts, may wish to be a bit more cautious in what it portends to promise its respective clientele. Arguably, both communities have much to offer. Yet as illustrated, performance gains rarely if ever accrue as rapidly or at the order of magnitude that is so often promised or advertised.

Summary

Performance gains accrue primarily through a series of incremental Type I innovations within a particular lineage. Such innovations commonly have a fairly high initial improvement frequency at the beginning of a new lineage, often exhibiting a positive exponent increase with compound growth (the steep part of the S-curve). Within this Type I innovation-dominated high-frequency phase, however, individual performance gains generally remain relatively small. Yet, in some instances, fairly substantial within-lineage performance gains occur as well.

Given enough time, Type I innovations almost always eventually stagnate and begin to stall out. Such slowing in incremental improvement frequency and resultant gains in performance results in a curve that begins to flatten abruptly, now representing a negative exponent increase and the initial formation of the top of the S. In this more mature phase, few performance gains accrue and the lineage becomes more or less stagnant, at least from a performance growth perspective.

In such mature growth situations, performance gains seem to be able to begin anew only through the introduction of a new innovation and the resultant creation of a new lineage. The start of this new lineage in turn often leads to a new round of incremental Type I innovations that in turn continue to accrue gains in performance. Accordingly, Type II, III, or IV innovations tend to beget Type I innovations. Type I innovations in turn result in incremental gains in performance (at least for a while).

The introduction of multiple innovations often creates a series of overlapping S-curves. In such instances, a new innovation represents the start of a new lineage that transforms into a new S-curve via renewed incremental gains in performance. This overlapping S-curve shape is dependent, however, on the following: (1) the new innovation actually being adopted by enough people to sustain the innovation, and (2) the innovation resulting in actual gains in performance.

Chapter 5

Modeling Performance

The June 11, 2007, cover of *BusinessWeek* magazine featured the head of a man wearing stylish, dark-rimmed glasses. The head, however, was completely obscured by overlapping, multi-colored sticky Post-it® notes made by 3M. On each note was written a phrase or acronym, like *DMAIC*, *Fishbone diagram*, *Mistake proofing*, or *Tollgate review*. Stuck under the left lens of the man's glasses was a Post-it note bearing the words *Regression analysis*. Under the right lens is another note containing $Y = f(x)$. Each of the written Post-it notes referred to nomenclature commonly associated with Six Sigma, a quality and efficiency process improvement methodology.

The magazine's front-cover headline of "3M's INNOVATION CRISIS" was printed above the note-plastered head in large, yellow-text letters against a black background. The sub-headline read, "How Six Sigma Almost Smothered Its Idea Culture." Reading the featured article entitled "At 3M, A Struggle between Efficiency and Creativity" and a shorter associated article entitled "Six Sigma: So Yesterday? In an Innovation Economy, It's No Longer a Cure-all," readers may have come away thinking that this $Y = f(x)$ stuff is not all that it is cracked up to be.

The gist of the two articles is that the Six Sigma–based drive to become more efficient at 3M, the birthplace of such innovative marvels as masking tape, Thinsulate, and Post-it notes, may be destroying its former creative- and innovative-based company self. Apparently, the quest to do things better, faster, and cheaper is significantly impeding the equally important need at 3M to do things in a more creative and innovative fashion.

Referring to Chapter 2, where I first introduced the $Y = f(x)$ formula, I noted that performance outcome Y is often driven by a few critical oomph factors. Remembering the Human Development Index (HDI) example, recall that the primary factors driving HDI are as follows:

- A *long and healthy life*, as measured by life expectancy at birth
- *Knowledge*, as measured by adult literacy rate (representing a two-thirds weighting) and the combined primary, secondary, and tertiary gross school enrollment ratios (representing a one-third weighting)
- A *decent standard of living*, as measured by per capita gross domestic product (GDP), normalized to U.S. dollar equivalents

As illustrated by HDI and many other examples, performance is often determined by just a few key factors. But there are *always* a few. Performance is a multi-dimensional phenomenon: it never seems to be a single-dimensional phenomenon determined by only a single oomph factor. Instead, one key performance factor always seems to have at least a few other key factors around for company. To more correctly express this multi-factor performance reality, perhaps the $Y = f(x)$ formula should be formulated as $Y = f(x\text{'s})$, indicating that the x part of the formula is always plural, containing more than a single x factor.

Returning to 3M, a simple performance model might suggest that 3M must successfully create stuff, make stuff, *and* sell stuff. Note that I did not write create, make, *or* sell stuff, but used the word *and*. Referring back to the *BusinessWeek* article, it is suggested that Six Sigma certainly has a great deal of application in helping 3M *make* stuff better, faster, and cheaper. But Six Sigma may have little application in assisting 3M in *creating* stuff better.

This does not mean, as the article implies to some, that Six Sigma is necessarily a bad tool and should be instantly abandoned. Rather, it means that Six Sigma is *only* a tool and needs to be judiciously and intelligently applied. A hammer is certainly a good tool. But we all know that a hammer cannot be used to build or fix everything, although some may try. Just like a hammer, Six Sigma needs to be applied and used for the right application in the right manner.

Accordingly, it is argued that there is nothing wrong with the $Y = f(x)$ formula. In the case of 3M, the company may have simply overfocused on one of the x's at the expense of other, equally critical and important x's. 3M's performance model may have become a bit skewed in its quest for achieving greater efficiency at the expense of the equally important variables of innovation and creativity.

The Dilemma of Safety versus Productivity

This single-dimensional and often myopic approach to performance modeling and associated performance management and improvement efforts is a fairly common and unfortunate phenomenon. In the summer of 2006, for example, the oil industry, propelled by record oil prices, was booming. Big and small companies alike were making lots of money and enjoying record profitability. But for every generalization, there is always an exception, and in the summer of 2006, that exception was British Petroleum (BP).

BP was rocked by an earlier catastrophic explosion at its Texas City refinery and a major oil spill of some 270,000 gallons in March 2006 that ultimately forced the company to shut down 400,000 barrels of daily oil production from its Alaska North Slope operation due to a faulty and corroded pipeline system. Since then, things just seemed to be getting worse. Accused of optimizing productivity and profitability at the expense of safety, BP suffered investigation after investigation.

Perhaps the crowning blow came when BP's top executives were forced to endure a humiliating and embarrassing trip to Capitol Hill. During a heated exchange of words on September 7, 2006, the U.S. Congress openly and very publicly berated BP as a stumbling, arrogant, irresponsible, and decidedly unsafe corporation.

What ultimately caused such damning accusations and BP's loss of public trust may perhaps be at least partially explained in an insightful book entitled *Managing the Risks of Organizational Accidents* by James Reason. In his book, Reason presents an informative and insightful graph that plots protection on one side and production on the other. The graph essentially represents a two-dimensional performance model for high-risk, hazardous operations like those conducted by BP.

According to Reason, if a company focuses *only* on protection at the expense of productivity, then it may eventually suffer bankruptcy. Conversely, if it focuses solely on production at the exclusion of protection or safety, then it can experience an equally unwanted catastrophic accident (such as BP's refinery explosion and pipeline spill). Thus, the challenge facing any company, according to Reason, is to plot and maintain a delicate path that appropriately balances protection and production.

As illustrated in Figure 5.1, a dual goal of many companies is to achieve simultaneous excellence via increasing productivity and improving safety. In truth, however, in order to be successful, companies must often balance these competing and conflicting goals. In some instances, companies must sacrifice productivity for safety. In other instances, however, they must attain required

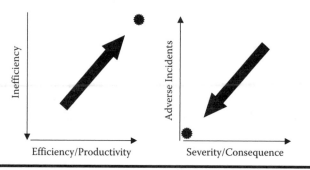

Figure 5.1   A depiction of the dual and often competing corporate performance goals of increasing productivity while significantly decreasing the number, severity, and associated consequence of adverse incidents (by improving safety).

productivity levels within the confines of an acceptable, yet certainly not risk-free safety envelope.

As illustrated in Figure 5.1, performance is never an *either/or* system but an *and* system. Performance is always multi-dimensional, and any constructed performance model must depict this multi-dimensional reality. Although such models may include only a few key dimensions, they always include a few. Accordingly, learning how to develop multi-dimensional models is a critical first step in better understanding, measuring, improving, and ultimately successfully managing performance irrespective of specific domain or venue.

Models: Definitions and Characteristics

As described in an article by Work and Balmforth and expanded upon in an excellent book by Gale and Eldred entitled *Getting Results with the Object-Oriented Enterprise Model*, you can formulate a definition of modeling via the concept of *abstraction*. Using this abstraction-based concept, modeling may be defined as a tool used to make sense of something that we *don't* understand in terms of something that we *do* understand. The thing that we don't understand is the often complex, messy, and fuzzy real world. What we do understand (or at least sort of understand) is the modeled world.

In modeling-speak, the *target system* represents what we don't understand but want to understand. What we do understand or partially understand is the *model system*. According to Work and Balmforth (1993), "Modeling postulates a similarity of structure between two items—the thing that is to be represented and the thing that serves as the model."

Models are ideally built by *observing* and *measuring* the real or target system. In turn, such observation- and measurement-based constructed models are used to *predict* the target system. I describe in greater detail how to go about observing and measuring systems in the following sections and in Chapters 6 and 7. For now, it is simply enough to note that people develop models or abstractions based primarily on observing and measuring real systems. In turn, such constructed abstractions or models can help you better predict what may occur in real-world systems.

Gale and Eldred expand in their book a bit more on this idea that models represent abstractions. According to the two authors, abstraction means "drawing out the essence of something." In developing any model then, you start with something familiar and attempt to draw out its essence. You use what is familiar and well known to analyze what is unknown and unfamiliar. More specifically, you develop a set of *principles* and *concepts* from the familiar world to analyze and better understand the unfamiliar and unknown world. According to Gale and Eldred, "a principle or concept that applies in the familiar world should also apply in the unfamiliar world we are striving to understand."

A common technique routinely used in developing a model is that of *decomposition.* To decompose something is to break that something down into its component elements or simpler constituents. Using an object-oriented language, modeling attempts to decompose a real or target system into higher-level *component objects.* In turn, higher-level component objects are decomposed into *sub-objects.* Additionally, sub-objects can be decomposed into *elements* and even associated *sub-elements.* This component object, sub-object, element, and sub-element decomposition framework is graphically illustrated in Figure 5.2. As shown in the figure, the end result of any decomposition effort is often a *hierarchical-type model* that can be disaggregated from the top down and re-aggregated from the bottom up.

Referencing the work of Bapat (1994), "the model defines clearly separated components on which we can focus our attention separately and sequentially." Yet we must never forget that these separated components also create a whole. Bapat recognizes the importance of the whole when he further notes that a model, "describes not only the components which result from such a decomposition but also the relationships of these components which describe how they interact to create the entire system."

Accordingly, the real goal of any modeling effort is to attempt to develop a mega-view of the target system or the *whole.* Such a mega-view represents the *architecture* of any system. Bapat states that, "architecture imposes an organization on the elements of a problem domain." Architecture, therefore, provides a way of "recognizing the major components of a system and the parameters under which they operate."

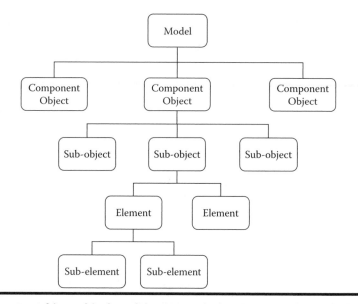

Figure 5.2   A hierarchical model composed of component objects, sub-objects, elements, and sub-elements.

A well-developed model serves many purposes. On one level, a model takes a complex real world and attempts to decompose that world into a series of elemental component objects. Yet a model must also show how the individual components or objects fit together and interact between and among each other. Good models are like a zoom lens on a camera, providing both a wide-angle whole view as well as a series of more detailed close-up shots.

Referring once again to the Human Development Index (HDI) example, a long and healthy life, knowledge, and a decent standard of living represent component objects of HDI. Conversely, the elements that affect a long and healthy life, such as infant, adolescent, and maternal mortality, represent sub-objects. Thus, we can speak in terms of a global HDI model that is decomposed into component objects that, in turn, are further broken down into individual sub-objects. You want to be able to think about and view any model from both top down (global model → component objects → sub-objects) and bottom up (sub-objects → component objects → global model).

Our particular interest here is in how to create performance models. A *performance model* in this newly developed object-oriented terminology is simply a particular type of model that attempts to identify the key component objects, sub-objects, elements, and sub-elements, along with their corresponding inter-actions and interrelations that drive or determine some wanted or unwanted performance outcome *Y*. In the following section, I will explore performance models in greater depth.

Performance Models

Numerous examples of performance models are found in the literature. Blumberg and Pringle (1982), for instance, developed a rather generic performance model that attempts to identify the key determinants governing work performance. At the highest level, their model consists of three component objects: *capacity* (*C*), *willingness* (*W*), and *opportunity* (*O*). These three component objects in turn can be translated into the following $Y = f(x)$ formula: work performance = $f(C \times W \times O)$.

In turn, you can decompose each of the component objects into sub-objects. *Capacity* is thus further decomposed into things like intelligence, learned skills, and physical fitness. *Willingness* refers to motivational and attitudinal factors that allow a person to use his or her capacities to full advantage, or alternatively, hinder him or her in fulfilling his or her potential. Finally, *opportunity* refers to things like the physical and social environment provided by the organization. An interactive-type hierarchical model for *work performance* is graphically illustrated in Figure 5.3.

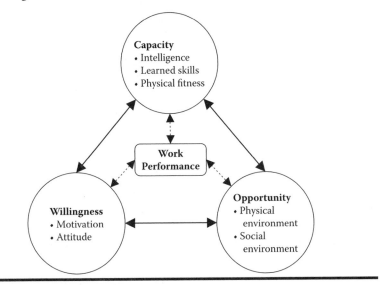

Figure 5.3   A model of work performance adapted from Blumberg and Pringle (1982) comprised of the component objects capacity, willingness, and opportunity and associated sub-objects.

As illustrated in Figure 5.3, work performance represents the interaction between and among these three top-level component objects. Although capacity, willingness, and opportunity are individually important components, it is their interaction (that is, their combined effect) that actually determines performance outcomes in the workplace. A person might have all the willingness in the world, but if he completely lacks the requisite capacity to perform, then his performance, despite his most willing efforts, is severely limited at best.

By comparison, Powers and Howley (2007) offer a more individual- and physiological-based model of human performance. According to the authors, human performance is a function of such component objects as diet, central nervous system function, strength/skill, environment, and energy production (including both anaerobic and aerobic sources).

In turn, each component object is further decomposed into sub-objects. Environment, for example, is decomposed into (1) altitude, (2) heat, and (3) humidity. Conversely, strength/skill is decomposed into (1) practice and (2) natural endowment. Additionally, the sub-object natural endowment is further decomposed into the elements (1) body type and (2) muscle fiber type.

In their book entitled *Exercise Physiology*, Powers and Howley also describe another performance-related model that identifies factors specifically affecting physical performance. In this more detailed and physical performance-related model, identified component objects include (1) coordination and economy, (2) environment, (3) psychological factors, (4) strength, and (5) energy output. Energy output is further decomposed into (1) aerobic and (2) anaerobic. Note both the similarities and differences between the two physiological-based models developed by Powers and Howley.

As illustrated and irrespective of subject matter or particular domain, most performance models follow the same decomposition-based methodology described. Higher-level component objects are decomposed into mid-level sub-objects. Mid-level sub-objects, in turn, are decomposed into yet lower-level elements and sub-elements.

Note also that there are two basic types of performance models: generic and specific. The work performance model of Blumberg and Pringle and the human performance models of Powers and Howley are good examples of *generic* models that apply equally well to almost any setting or domain. Yet, in many instances, you may wish to create a performance model that specifically applies to a particular domain or application area.

A good example of a domain-specific model is one developed by Berri, Schmidt, and Brook in reference to basketball. According to the authors, a very simple model of basketball team wins can be summarized with the logic statement: Wins are solely a function of offensive and defensive efficiency. In other words, basketball wins are determined solely by what you do when your team possesses the ball and what you do when the other team possesses the ball.

In the object-oriented nomenclature, offensive and defensive efficiency represent component objects. Basically, if component object offensive efficiency is greater than component object defensive efficiency, your team wins. If not, your team loses!

In turn, the component object offensive efficiency, measured by points scored per possession employed (that is, what your team does when it has the ball), is further decomposed into sub-objects like field goal attempts made, free throw attempts made, turnovers, and offensive rebounds. Conversely, defensive efficiency, measured by points allowed per possession acquired (or what your team does when the other team has the ball), is further decomposed into the sub-objects of opponent turnovers, defensive rebounds, team rebounds, opponent-made field goal attempts, and opponent-made free throw attempts.

You may wish to further determine the interaction among these various component objects and sub-objects. Often, such identified interactions are counterintuitive. For example, you might think that offensive rebounds are a good thing. Yet the more offensive rebounds that a team accrues, the more times they missed a shot. Higher offensive rebounding numbers are actually correlated with poor shooting numbers that, in turn, are correlated with a greater number of games lost.

This admittedly brief introduction to modeling is further explored in the following section in a fairly detailed case study on how to actually build a performance model.

Modeling Case Study

Each year the Department of Energy (DOE) hosts a special competition among its elite security forces that are charged with protecting materials, people, and facilities at its various sites. Currently called Security Protection Officer Training Competition (SPOTC), the competition is also open to law enforcement SWAT-type teams, as well as special tactical or close quarter battle (CQB) military units.

The demanding, almost weeklong competition, which is normally held in late spring or early summer, has earned the justifiable reputation of being a premiere tactical shooting event. This well-earned national and increasingly international recognition is due in large part to the incredible effort put forth by the remarkable men and women of the Department of Energy's National Training Center, who sponsor, develop, coordinate, and run SPOTC each year.

SPOTC consists of both individual events in which competitors must compete on their own, and team events composed of five-person teams (or stacks).

For the 2007 competition, there were five individual events, five team events, and one super-team event.

Each event consists of a specific course of fire on a separate firing range (except for the super-team event, which occurs over multiple ranges). A course of fire consists of one or more stages and associated painted metal target sets. Target sets contain both shoot targets and orange- and yellow-painted no-shoot targets.

Further, each individual stage consists of one or more firing positions. At numerous stages, competitors must successfully hit (literally knocking down) one set of metal targets before immediately changing positions and firing at another set of targets Additionally, on some courses of fire, competitors are required to go over, under, or through various types of obstacles when moving from one stage to another.

Some events or courses of fire are rifle only, meaning that competitors fire only their standard-issued M-4 carbine. Other events are pistol or handgun only. Still other events are both rifle and handgun, requiring the transition from one weapon type to another. The good news about SPOTC compared to other shooting events is that competitors can carry as much ammo as they want. Consequently, SPOTC represents a multi-day competition that entails lots of firing at lots of targets and the expenditure of literally thousands of rounds of ammunition.

At some stages, competitors are required to don a gas mask and fire at targets with their faces covered. During the 2007 super-team event, teams also had to run to and from one stage while wearing a gas mask. This gas-donning requirement in the super-team event immediately followed running from one range to an adjacent range, all at some 6,000-foot elevation. Obviously SPOTC is not for the faint of heart or poorly conditioned!

Competitors in both the individual and team event competitions are scored by how long it takes them to complete a specific event. Depending on the type of event and what is involved, winning times can vary widely. In the 2007 competition, for example, winning times in the individual events ranged from some 62 to 75 seconds. Conversely, in the team events, winning scores ranged from a low of 22 seconds to a high of 250 seconds for the demanding and longer super-team event.

The goal of SPOTC is to complete each event in as little time as possible without incurring any additional time penalties. For example, if a shoot target is left standing at the end of an event, or a no-shoot target is incorrectly hit, a so-called procedural, representing a 10- or 30-second time penalty, is added to an individual's or team's score. A winning strategy is thus to complete a particular course of fire as fast as possible without incurring any penalties. The end of an event occurs either when the last-standing green-painted stop plate (or target) is hit, or when the allotted and allowable time for that particular event has expired.

Because SPOTC scores are in seconds, you can state that outcome Y is represented by event completion time, as measured in seconds. This time-dependent outcome is expressed in the $Y = f(x)$ formula as *seconds* = $f(x)$. The fewer seconds accrued, the greater the probability of a winning time. SPOTC is thus essentially a race against the clock. Yet speed is always tempered by shooting accuracy.

Having first identified the outcome Y as represented by seconds, you must now turn your attention to identifying our critical x's (top-level component objects). From the previous discussion of modeling, you know that a model is often built by observing and measuring the real world. In the case of SPOTC, observing the various events reveals that contestants are basically doing as follows:

- Shooting at targets (and not shooting at no-shoot targets).
- Moving from one shooting position to another within various stages
- Moving between stages, often over, under, or through various types of obstacles.
- Loading, unloading, and reloading weapons.
- Donning gas masks (sometimes).
- For team events, coordinating actions and communicating (actually, shouting) directions; the shouting is almost always done by the team's captain.

Based on such observational data, you could begin to build a performance model composed of the actions of shooting, moving, and shouting. Note, however, that shooting, moving, and shouting are what they are *doing*. That is, shooting, moving, and shouting are the tasks that are actually being performed. If we wish to build a performance model as opposed to a task-based model, you must identify what it is about shooting, moving, and communicating that directly affects performance as measured by outcome Y, here measured in seconds.

In the case of shooting, it is the *accuracy* of shooting that affects Y: the fewer bullets or rounds expended per target, the fewer number of seconds that accrue. As one person succinctly put it, "You simply can't miss fast enough to win a SPOTC event." Greater accuracy thus equals less time.

In terms of movement, it is the *speed of movement* that counts. The faster one moves within and between stages, the faster one completes the various events. This faster observation, however, is always tempered by the need to also successfully hit the targets at each stage. Accordingly, there is a very strong interaction between accuracy and speed of movement. Fast or speed of movement counts, but being accurate *and* fast counts much more.

There is also a very strong cognitive or decision-making component as well, as represented by selected tactics, shoot/no-shoot decisions, and coordination and communication in team events. As such, you can identify *cognition* as a third critical component. Thus the high-level shoot, move, and shout task model is now translated into a more representative and meaningful accuracy, speed of movement, and cognition performance model. This performance-based representation is captured by the formula: seconds = f(accuracy × speed of movement × cognition).

As illustrated in Figure 5.4, this global SPOTC performance model is composed of three principle component objects or oomph factors: accuracy, speed of movement, and cognition. These three component objects are applicable to both individual and teams events. However, depending on the specific individual or team event in question, one top-level factor or component object may account for greater variance in outcome performance, as measured in seconds, than does another component object.

For example, because of the long distances between individual stages in the super-team event, speed of movement becomes much more important for that event. Conversely, in other events comprised of only a single-stage, or in events in which interstage distances are relatively short, accuracy is the dominant component object.

You can further translate the component objects speed of movement, accuracy, and cognition into more specific performance improvement factors. There are multiple physiological, skill, and cognitive factors associated with improving speed of movement, accuracy, and cognition, respectively. These improvement-related factors are more fully addressed in Chapter 7.

To continue the SPOTC performance modeling effort, you must next decompose each component object into various sub-objects. For example, you can decompose the component object speed of movement into the sub-objects (1) intrastage and (2) interstage. In turn, the two elements that most affect speed of movement at the interstage level are the distance between the stages (that is, the greater the distance between two stages, the more important that speed of

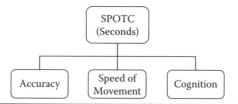

Figure 5.4 An initial SPOTC hierarchical model comprised of the component objects accuracy, speed of movement, and cognition.

movement becomes) and the number, type, and associated level of difficulty of obstacles that must be surmounted between stages.

Thus, in the emerging SPOTC performance model, distance and obstacles are elements of the sub-object interstage. In turn, interstage is a sub-object of the higher-level component object speed of movement. In any modeling effort, you can decompose a model from top to bottom, as well as recompose it (or aggregate it) from bottom to top.

At the intrastage sub-object level, a number of factors affect speed of movement, including the following: number of required shooting position transitions (the time required to move from one shooting position to another within an individual stage), target acquisition (the amount of time required to acquire, aim, and engage a target), equipment retrieval and storage (the time required to retrieve weapons and additional magazines, and retrieve and store gas masks and personal protection equipment), and weapon manipulation (the time required to load, unload, and reload weapons and clear any jammed rounds if necessary).

Based on such identified factors, a first cut for the component object speed of movement and its decomposed sub-objects and associated elements is illustrated in Figure 5.5. Note that modeling is and always should be an iterative process. Accordingly and as illustrated in Figure 5.5, first attempts should always be viewed as just that—first attempts.

Perhaps one of the most useful aspects of modeling is that after you commit a graphical model to paper or some other electronic medium, and no matter how crude and incomplete it is, you can instantly start playing with it and see what

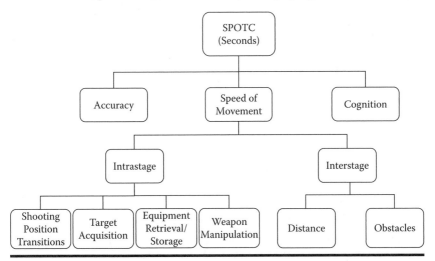

Figure 5.5   The further decomposition of the component object speed of movement.

insights you might derive. Of particular importance in such exploration-based ventures is better understanding how component objects, sub-objects, and elements might interact and interrelate between and among each other.

For example, if you ponder Figure 5.5 a bit, you might observe that accuracy has no effect on interstage speed of movement. Because competitors are not shooting as they move between stages, accuracy is not a compounding factor (it does not affect interstage accrued time).

Conversely, accuracy directly affects intrastage speed of movement. Greater accuracy at an individual stage means that fewer rounds are fired. Fewer rounds fired directly translate into the fewer times contestants have to retrieve a fresh magazine and reload their weapon.

Retrieving a fresh magazine and reloading a weapon consumes precious seconds. Accuracy thus directly translates into fewer seconds consumed. Fewer seconds consumed in turn translates into a better performance outcome Y. As illustrated, the component object accuracy *does* affect speed of movement in a number of ways at the intrastage sub-object level. Yet as also illustrated, accuracy *does not* affect speed of movement at the interstage sub-object level.

In building any performance model, it is important to identify not only individual component objects and sub-objects comprising the model, but also the interrelation and interaction between and among those objects. In some instances one identified object may not affect another object (for example, accuracy does not affect interstage speed of movement). Conversely, in many other instances, one object does affect another object in either a positive or negative manner (for example, accuracy directly affects intrastage speed of movement in both a positive and negative manner). Accordingly, it is critical to identify both objects and the interrelationships between and among those identified objects when building any performance model.

Such insights can in turn be translated into a set of associated model rules. For example:

Rule 1: The fewer rounds expended, the greater the accuracy. The greater the accuracy, the fewer seconds accrued.

Rule 2: The component object accuracy directly affects speed of movement for sub-object intrastage.

Rule 3: The component object accuracy does not affect speed of movement for sub-object interstage.

Rule 4: The greater the distance between stages, the greater the performance effect of sub-object interstage on outcome Y.

The construction of such model-related rule sets forces you to explicitly state how objects interact and interrelate between and among each other. Often surprising and sometimes even counterintuitive insights are gained during the generation of model-related rule sets.

To initially complete the SPOTC performance model, you can further decompose the component objects accuracy and cognition. For example, you could decompose the component object accuracy into two sub-objects labeled *rifle* and *handgun*. Additionally, you could decompose cognition into the sub-objects individual and team.

In Chapters 6 and 7, you will discover that this initial decomposition effort is inadequate for our needs in terms of understanding, measuring, and improving performance. Consequently, you will need to do a bit more decomposition-related work later. For now, however, and as illustrated in Figure 5.6, this is not too bad of start for this first SPOTC performance modeling attempt.

In reading this section, you may disagree with the developed performance model and initial decomposition attempt that I have rendered. Ideally, a model serves two purposes: as an abstraction of the real world and as a communication tool. Whether you agree or disagree with my initial modeling and associated decomposition efforts, the derived model has forced you to critically think about what *is* (and just as importantly what *isn't*) driving performance in this particular event-based domain. And in the end, that may be the real value of any modeling effort: to force people to critically think about what is and is not driving performance.

If you wish to proceed further with this modeling effort, you may want to translate this developed graphical model into a more mathematical-based model via regression analysis or some other selected mathematical modeling technique. For this example, however, I have kept things fairly simple and have ended here.

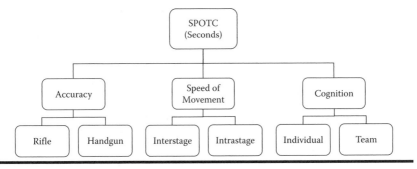

Figure 5.6   An initial SPOTC performance model decomposed only to the sub-object level.

Outlining the Case Study Steps

With the SPOTC case study, I hope I have illustrated that with a bit of critical thinking and associated real-world observation, anyone can develop a performance model such as illustrated in Figures 5.4–5.6. To review the critical steps in developing a performance-based model, we:

1. Described and developed an initial understanding of the domain to be modeled (that is, understanding what SPOTC is all about).

2. Identified outcome Y (Y equals actual start-stop event times measured in seconds plus any additional accrued time penalties, also measured in seconds).

3. Observed the various events, identifying what was actually happening (people were shooting, moving, and communicating).

4. Translated these observed key actions (or what was happening) into critical x performance factors. These identified critical factors became our high-level component objects (for example, accuracy, speed of movement, and cognition).

5. Decomposed these higher-level component objects into sub-objects. For example, the component object speed of movement was decomposed into two sub-objects: intrastage movement and interstage movement. This decomposition effort continued, further dividing each sub-object into lower elemental objects (for example, equipment retrieval and storage).

6. Thought about the interrelation and interaction among our identified objects (such as the fact that accuracy affects intrastage movement but not interstage movement). This thought process captured these various observed interactions in a preliminary set of model-related rules.

And that is it: six fairly easy steps. Although you can certainly make our constructed performance models more complex, in any modeling effort, the real goal is to capture the true essence of a particular performance domain. In many instances, simple really is better and is almost always easier to understand.

The Value of Performance Modeling

You may be asking, "But what is the real value of such performance modeling efforts?" Modeling can help you better understand, measure, improve, and manage performance. But perhaps more importantly, models can also help you compete in often new, different, and in many instances, decidedly cheaper ways.

Value to the Oakland A's

Chapter 2 describes how the low-budget Oakland Athletics essentially created a new model (admittedly based on the previous pioneering work of others) for valuing, acquiring, and managing Major League Baseball players. But how successful is their so-called different and cheaper model when compared to the "spend as much money as you possibly can to buy the best players possible" model of the New York Yankees?

Examining only normal season play from 2000 to 2006, the mighty New York Yankees won 679 games and lost 451 games. Over seven full seasons of play, the Yanks won 60.09 percent of their games.

By contrast and over the exact same time period, the Oakland Athletics won 664 games and lost 469 games. In total then, the A's won 58.61 percent of their games, just 1.48 percent shy of the Yankees' 60.09 percent average. From this brief analysis, it is difficult to draw any definitive conclusions on who has the better model; it appears to be essentially a draw with no real observed significant differences. So, from only a winning percentage or performance outcome perspective, one model seems about as good as the other model.

Conversely, when you look at total salaries spent over that same seven-season period, you observe some very real differences. The mighty and decidedly richer Yankees spent about a billion dollars ($1,071,067,646) on player salaries over the covered time period. This works out to an individual average per game cost of $947,843. If you look only at what it costs to win a game for the Yanks and completely ignore the cost of losing, then the price tag escalates to $1,577,419 per game won.

Viewing once again the same seven-season time period, the Oakland A's spent a total of $333,292,092. In turn this works out to an individual per game cost of $294,167. If you calculate only what it costs to win a game and completely ignore what it costs to lose a game, as done previously with the Yanks, the price tag for the A's increases to $501,945 per game won.

You can further illustrate this disparity in salaries between the two ball clubs by focusing exclusively on the 2002 baseball season. During the 2002 season, Oakland and New York won the exact same number of games, 103. They also both lost their initial American League division playoff games, the Yankees losing to Anaheim and Oakland losing to Minnesota.

Figure 5.7 plots total 2002 salaries versus total wins for all Major League Baseball teams. Note once again that although the A's and Yankees have the best season win records, they had decidedly different salary costs associated with those per game wins.

From such analyses it might be safe to conclude that the A's have reached an amazing performance or competitive parity with the higher-priced Yankees.

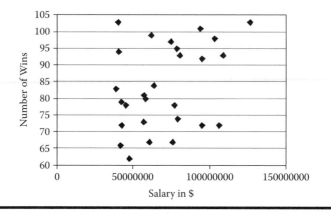

Figure 5.7   A graphical plot of Major League Baseball team salaries versus total team wins for the 2002 regular baseball season. Note the two top teams with the greatest number of wins are the cheaper Oakland A's on the left and the decidedly more expensive New York Yankees on the right.

Although the Yanks spend on average about 3.2 times more each season than the A's, the end result (the *Y* value in terms of games won at least in the regular season) is about the same. Conversely, if you look only at cost-to-performance outcome ratios, you could argue that Oakland is by far the superior team. This cost-to-performance outcome ratio perspective for the described 2002 season differentiated a number of other Major League Baseball teams as well. As such, performance models really do matter, especially when achieving performance parity at much lower costs.

In all fairness to the New York Yankees, the above analysis focuses only on the marginal cost of winning. It does not take into account the marginal revenue generated from winning. For an excellent discussion of marginal revenue from winning versus the marginal cost of winning, check out Vince Gennaro's insightful book entitled *Diamond Dollars—The Economics of Winning in Baseball*.

As illustrated then, you can often equal the playing field and attain reasonable and sometimes even startling performance parity simply by creating a different, if not better and often cheaper, performance model. This observation is as applicable to the sports world as it is to the business world. It also, unfortunately, is equally applicable to the war or military world.

Value to the U.S. Military

Indeed, this concept of achieving parity via differing cost-to-performance outcome ratios is perhaps nowhere more evident than in the current U.S. military situation. As described by Max Boot (in an absolutely fascinating article entitled

"The Paradox of Military Technology" that appeared in the Fall 2006 issue of *The New Atlantis*, a journal devoted exclusively to exploring the interaction between technology and society), the U.S. military finds itself in a rather paradoxical position. On the one hand, we live in an age of U.S. military supremacy little matched in the annals of world history.

As supporting evidence for this observation, our aircraft carrier–led task groups surrounded by Ticonderoga-class cruisers, Arleigh Burke–class destroyers, and nuclear-powered attack submarines dominate the open blue water to such an extent that no one even attempts to challenge the might of the U.S. Navy on the open seas anymore. In point of fact, the last major ship-to-ship battle took place in 1944 in the Leyete Gulf, a body of water located immediately east of the island of Leyete in the Philippines.

In the air, the United States holds a similar dominant position. Although Boot cautions that all aircraft are vulnerable to advanced surface-to-air missile (SAM) threats, U.S. fighter, bomber, and transport planes have not been seriously challenged by a foe's air assets for decades. To illustrate this aerial dominance, the Air Force has not produced a single ace (an airman with at least five kills) since 1972. Neither has the U.S. military suffered a single soldier death from enemy air action since the Korean conflict.

In space, growing numbers of surveillance, communications, and other satellite platforms provide the United States with an eye and ear in the sky presence that clearly dominates over any other country's space assets. As such, the U.S. military clearly owns the global commons of open water, open air, and open space.

In land warfare, the the U.S. military possesses probably the best main battle tank in the world, the M1 Abrams. Yet other battle tanks, including the British Challenger II, the German Leopold II, the Russian T-80 and T-90, and the Israeli Merkava Mk4, are formidable contenders for this "world best" title.

Our existing land warfare vehicle- and artillery-based arsenal is currently being augmented by a slew of proposed lightweight and more mobile manned and unmanned ground combat vehicles under the Future Combat System (FCS) program. The Future Combat System program will further network an unprecedented array of unattended ground sensors and unmanned aerial vehicle (UAV) platforms as well. The ultimate goal of such advanced, network-centric combat warfare systems is to finally remove the often-cited Clausewitzian fog of war.

For a time being at least, and as successfully demonstrated during the opening months of Operation Enduring Freedom in Afghanistan, this military-technical revolution, which combines U.S. airpower, precision-guided munitions (PGMs), space and UAV surveillance assets, and special operations ground forces marking targets with high-tech lasers for precision aerial strike, seems to represent a true revolution in techno-centric warfare. By clearly demonstrating such overwhelming technological prowess and air superiority, some argue that the U.S. military had finally reached a position such that, in future conflicts, it could greatly limit the number of combat troops committed on the ground, if not outright eliminate fielding traditional armies almost completely.

Yet today, on the other hand, this predicted revolution in techno-centric warfare has not materialized to the extent forecasted or envisioned by many of its proponents. And thus the paradox described by Boot: that modern technology is both "the great separator and the equalizer in military affairs." Although technology supremacy separates the United States from the rest of the world, readily available modern technology in the hands of nonstate and state aggressors alike also leaves the U.S. military vulnerable, creating what some have called a *battlefield counterrevolution*.

To further highlight this so-called technology paradox, headlines increasingly proclaim that low-tech insurgents are foiling today's high-tech militaries. A more apt headline may be that locally adapted, right-tech-equipped insurgents are increasingly challenging today's high-tech military might. A major reason for this observed dissonance is that we often confuse technological superiority with performance superiority.

It is suggested that what Boot describes as a technological paradox may, in fact, be more appropriately described as a performance paradox. Just as the Oakland A's successfully rethought the game of baseball, some U.S. foes are also creating new and innovative performance models based on cheaper yet still deadly technologies and associated tactics. They have, unfortunately, learned through trial and error that surprising performance parities can often be achieved against even the most advanced militaries of the world.

The Soviet-Afghan war in the 1980s, the summer 2006 Hezbollah-Israeli conflict in southern Lebanon, and at the time of this writing, the ongoing insurgency and outright civil war in Iraq, all represent examples of this emerging reality of cost to actual performance outcome.

During the Soviet-Afghan war in Afghanistan, for example, a country that is a bit smaller than Texas and characterized by flat topography to the west and mountainous terrain to the east, the Soviets enjoyed overwhelming air superiority—at least until 1986. Such dominant airpower was achieved by the Soviet's use of in-theater squadrons of MIG fighters, Su-25 Frogfoot ground attack aircraft, and Mi-24 Hind helicopter gunships.

The Mi-24 Hind helicopter gunship, armed with its turret-mounted four-barrel 12.7 mm Gatling-type machine guns, 57 mm rockets, and AT2-C/SWATTER anti-tank guided missiles (ATGMs), was especially feared by Afghan Mujahideen, and justifiably so. The Hind gunship, in combination with Soviet ground commandoes, effectively constrained and in some areas outright shutdown resupply routes along Afghan's porous eastern border with Pakistan. This deadly gunship-commando duo effectively deprived the Mujahideen of badly needed weapons, ammunition, and other war-related materials.

In 1986, however, situations changed markedly, and Soviet air prowess was effectively negated. This marked change was brought about mostly by the introduction of U.S.-supplied and primarily mule-transported, man-portable, shoulder-fired FIM-92A Stinger surface-to-air missiles, in combination with other types of anti-aircraft artillery. Regarding the Stinger missile, it is reported that the $60,000 Stinger successfully destroyed Soviet aircraft some 70 percent of the time, costing the Soviets literally millions of dollars in lost aircraft.

The deadly accuracy of the Stinger further forced Soviet Su-25 aircraft and Mi-24 helicopter pilots to fly above the effective range of surface-to-air missiles, thereby severely diminishing their effectiveness when compared to previously successful low-altitude air operations. Indeed, the Soviets learned the hard way that mules plus Stingers beat Hinds much of the time.

It is important to note that the primary effect of the Stinger missile success was the reopening of supply and transport networks based along the Pakistani border. With supply lines re-established, the war quickly turned against the Soviets. Weapons and resistance fighters alike freely entered Afghanistan via previously closed or severely constrained transport routes.

Although the Mujahideen did not necessarily achieve a technological superiority over the better-equipped Soviets, they did, via the Stinger and other tactical weapon systems, effectively level the playing field at least on a local scale. In turn, this leveling effect achieved a surprising performance parity that eventually resulted in the Soviet's withdrawing from Afghanistan. The lesson here is that if you cannot compete head on (or cannot afford to compete head on), get a different performance model!

The 2006 summer conflict in southern Lebanon pitting Syrian- and Iranian-backed Hezbollah guerilla forces against the vaunted Israeli Defense Force (IDF) was a far cry from Israel's prior military successes. Past Israeli wars featured massive pitched battles between tank formations that swept across flat, open, and relatively unobstructed desert terrain.

In the latest Lebanon conflict, however, the Israeli Army quickly became bogged down in the hilly and rugged terrain of southern Lebanon. Of particular significance is the observation that the local conditions of southern Lebanon made the latest generation of Israeli Merkava Mk4 tanks especially vulnerable to man- and crew-portable anti-tank guided missile and rocket-propelled grenade volleys fired by small teams of Hezbollah tank hunters.

As in the Afghanistan example, the effective use of leveling technologies combined with new performance models (that is, new tactics) adapted to local conditions proved extremely problematic for the better-equipped and technologically superior Israeli forces. The reader is once again reminded of the chilling al-Qaeda quote in Chapter 1 discussing how a rocket-propelled grenade (RPG) costing tens of dollars can destroy a $100 million tank! This statement represents a compelling reason why modern-day military strategists must fundamentally rethink the concepts of performance parity and associated cost-to-performance outcome ratio models when dealing with an increasingly asymmetrical warfare threat. Just as Stingers and mules beat Hinds in Afghanistan, other man-portable weapons effectively mitigated the technological superiority of Israeli Merkava Mk4 tanks in Lebanon.

Finally, the current post-war insurgency in Iraq demonstrates the risks posed to modern military forces and states by opponents that in Britain's Sir Rupert Smith's words "choose to fight below the threshold in which conventional armies are most effective," or in essence, adopt a different performance model. As we are learning in the case of the ongoing Iraqi insurgency, even comparatively small transfers of equalizer technologies, such as motion sensors, crude-shaped charges, and better triggering devices, can significantly increase the lethality and brutality of insurgent and terrorist organizations alike.

Indeed, it is argued that (1) easily transported but difficult to detect man- and crew-portable weapon systems such as anti-tank guided missiles, shoulder-fired surface-to-air missiles, advanced rocket-propelled grenades, and even small and easily purchased unmanned aerial vehicles, (2) when coupled with improvised explosive devices, shaped charges, and landmines, and (3) augmented by ubiquitous small arms like the AK-47 assault rifle, (4) place many groups, especially when fighting under local conditions in crowded and congested urban environments, on an essentially equal footing with even the most advanced armies of the world, including that of the United States.

Whether talking about sports, business, war, or just about anything else, performance models matter. Indeed, our ability to successfully discover the very essence of performance via creating new and different models often results in decidedly different results. Sometimes, the outcome in successfully discovering the essence of performance translates into a better result. At other times, however, it may result in essentially the same result, but at significantly less cost. Either way, the essence of x's matter. But as discussed in the following section, this statement is predicated on the fact that you first have to correctly discover the right set of x's!

Some Limitations of Performance Modeling

A well-constructed performance model represents significant utility and practical application. Yet like most things, performance models must be applied and used in a judicious manner. A few common performance model-related pitfalls are discussed in this section.

A model is and always will be just that: a model or an abstraction of the real world. The real world is real, while a model, no matter how well constructed, is not real. When a model is blindly and ignorantly substituted for reality, we are usually headed for trouble.

Models must be continuously updated and tinkered with. A good model may become a bad model at a later time if the real world changes significantly. This observation is particularly true with many business and military models. Selling individually customized computers directly to the buyer via just-in-time manufacturing techniques, for example, may have been a great business model. Yet changing customer buying habits can, through time, negate the utility of such direct-sales approaches. As the real world changes, so must our developed models change. You should never use yesterday's model to fight today's wars!

In any modeling effort, x's really do matter. Identifying the wrong x's, or those without any real oomph value, can seriously degrade a model's value and, in some instances, severely cost an organization in terms of both dollars and performance. This is where such mathematical techniques as regression analysis can really pay off. Regression analysis helps measure the specific contribution (or variance) that an individual x factor specifically contributes to outcome Y. In plain-speak, we need to avoid insignificant x's or those that simply do not matter.

Just as it is important to identify the right x's, it is equally important to identify the right Y's (outcomes). Answering the question "What really matters?" and rolling those answers into higher-level indexes like the Human Development Index is critical to any successful modeling effort.

Don't ever assume that your model is the only model possible. Just as there are supposedly many ways to skin a cat, so are there often multiple ways to achieve a particular performance outcome and associated performance parity. Although one model may not necessarily be any better than another model, it may be just as good, and often at significantly less cost.

It is suggested then that performance models have great utility. However, they also have admitted limitations. Recognizing a model's limitations is just as important as recognizing its value, and vice versa. Yet despite such recognized limitations, it is argued that well-constructed performance models, when judiciously and intelligently applied, do have significant value.

This proposition that models have value is especially true when you use performance models to assist you in determining what to measure and what and how to improve what you measure. Chapter 6 focuses on this question of what to measure.

Summary

A model represents an abstraction of the real world (that is, a target system). Accordingly, any developed model attempts to use the familiar to understand the unfamiliar. An effective way to build a model is via decomposition. Using an object-oriented language and approach, a model is decomposed into component objects. Component objects, in turn, are decomposed into sub-objects. Sub-objects can be further decomposed into elements and sub-elements.

Developed models can be either generic or specific in origin and application. A performance model is a generic or specific model that attempts to identify the key component objects, sub-objects, elements, and sub-elements, and associated interactions and interrelations that drive or determine some wanted or unwanted performance outcome Y.

A relatively easy-to-follow method for developing a performance model involves six iterative steps:

1. Developing an initial understanding of the subject domain to be modeled
2. Identifying outcome $Y(s)$
3. Observing/measuring the domain to be modeled
4. Identifying critical x's
5. Decomposing identified x's into component objects, sub-objects, elements, and sub-elements (if needed)
6. Developing a rule set that identifies significant interactions and interrelations between and among identified objects

Chapter 6

Measuring Performance

The time period is the early 1200s. The place is a vast kingdom located in a remote corner of Central Asia. Some 20 years earlier, you accepted the honored position of kingdom CPO (chief performance officer). Immediately upon assuming this highly respected and coveted position, you set about creating a kingdom-specific performance model. In the constructed model, one that is continuously refined and updated, you identified a limited set of key factors that affect overall kingdom success.

One identified critical factor (or component object) is food consumption. A hungry population can quickly turn into an unhappy and even violent one when food supplies become scarce. You reason, therefore, that at the most basic level, the kingdom must produce enough food to feed its population, if peace and order are to be maintained.

In turn, you decompose the component object food consumption into two sub-objects, food production and population. Via this relatively simple decomposition effort you have essentially developed a supply-and-demand-type performance model. That is, if food production exceeds population, supply exceeds demand and all is well. Conversely, if population exceeds food production, demand exceeds supply and, in this case, all is not well in the kingdom, and mouths outrun the food.

Each year in the late fall, after the annual harvest has been completed, you send what have become known as counters throughout the kingdom on foot and horseback to count and inventory food supplies and population. You then aggregate these individually collected counter numbers into overall kingdom totals. As illustrated in Figure 6.1, you plot both food consumption and population,

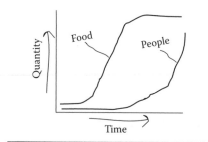

Figure 6.1 A crudely drawn graph plotting food production versus population growth. Despite the crudeness of the graph, a great deal of descriptive, predictive, and prescriptive information can be derived.

combining the two data sets onto a single, and admittedly crudely drawn, graph form. After compiling and plotting all collected data, you schedule an appointment to deliver the annual state of the kingdom performance report to the king and his court.

This year, based on the plotted data illustrated in Figure 6.1, you issue a dire warning that population growth may outpace food production in a few short years. Because the kingdom is geographically confined by a tall mountain range on one side and a barren and vast desert on the other, you have few realistic options to increase food production. Indeed, as noted in the depicted graph, food production essentially topped out some years ago and has not changed appreciably since. As such, there are few possibilities to significantly increase food production in the coming years.

Conversely, and as illustrated by the constructed graph, population continues to increase in a steep and inflationary growth form. You worry that within a few years population growth will exceed available food stocks. You and the king discuss alternatives and realize that there are very few. The kingdom must find a way to either: (1) significantly increase food supplies, which seems nearly impossible given the described geographical barriers bounding the kingdom; (2) ration available food supplies, an act that may create dissatisfaction and even possible unrest among the kingdom's population; or (3) somehow slow population growth, maintaining population size at a level that is constantly below available food stocks. The last alternative would seem to ensure an adequate food supply for the kingdom's inhabitants. After discussing the problem a bit with the king and his court, you come to the realization that option 3 is the only viable path forward if the kingdom is to achieve a maintainable and sustainable existence.

Although admittedly crudely drawn, Figure 6.1 provides an incredible wealth of performance-related information. First, it clearly describes what is and has been occurring in regard to both food production and population growth. Viewing the graph, one can easily grasp both historical and current trends in kingdom-related food production and population growth.

The plotted graphic also provides a great deal of predictive value. That is, it clearly shows that if the kingdom's population continues to grow at the current rate and food production holds steady, population growth will almost certainly exceed available food stocks sometime in the near future.

Finally, Figure 6.1 provides prescriptive value, allowing the viewer some diagnostic insights that can answer the question of "What can we do about the problem?" Seeing that food production is not increasing and that it has not been increasing for a number of years now, about the only variable that you can realistically affect or change is population growth.

As will be described in subsequent sections of this chapter, performance measures have many uses. Regardless of particular domain or types of measures employed, however, a good performance measurement system should always provide the following:

- Descriptive value, describing what is and has happened
- Predictive value, helping to extrapolate and translate past and present trends or single measures of performance into future possible trends and other measures of performance (particularly other outcome measures)
- Prescriptive value, assisting us in diagnosing potential performance-related problems and offering possible solutions, if any

In the following sections, I will explore this topic of performance measurement in greater detail, focusing in particular on how to better identify *what* to measure, how to select appropriate *units* of measurement, and how to better *interpret* what has been measured. Despite the large number of performance measurement–related books and published articles, these three basic subjects—what, unit, and interpretation—are often overlooked or inadequately addressed.

In this chapter, I also return to a case study from Chapter 5, involving a developed SPOTC performance model. But I start with a few performance measurement–related definitions and general observations that might aid subsequent discussions.

Some Definitions and General Observations about Performance Measures

Measurement involves ascertaining the size, amount, or degree of something. *Performance measurement* attempts to measure or ascertain either the outcomes of performance (value Y) or the *means* (x factors) that affect such outcomes. In turn, a *performance measurement system* involves the collection, synthesis, delivery, and graphical display of information related to these measures. Finally, a *performance metric* is simply a specific performance measure (such as cycle time).

Although there are many different types of performance measures, I will primarily focus on three: descriptive, predictive, and prescriptive measures. Note that in some instances, and depending on how such measures are graphically displayed, the same measure may serve all three functions.

Descriptive Measures

A *descriptive measure* describes what is happening or has happened. Such measures commonly depict a specific outcome and are often used to trend a particular phenomenon over time from a historical perspective. Accordingly, descriptive measures are also termed *lagging indicators*, indicating a predominantly backward or rearview-mirror view.

Figure 6.2 depicts a decreasing trend in the number of accidents occurring over time. Note from Figure 6.2 that although you can clearly see that the number of accidents has been steadily decreasing, you have no real way of knowing from the presented data the cause of the observed decrease or whether the decreasing trend will continue. Although descriptive measures often give you a good view of what is and has happened, they often fail to tell you why something is happening or what may subsequently happen in the future. These "what versus why" and "what may happen" limitations are particularly true when such measures are presented in isolation or do not evolve from a previously developed performance model (more on this in later sections of this chapter).

A series of descriptive performance measures, however, can often paint a detailed picture of what has and is happening in regard to a particular phenomenon. Figure 6.3, for example, depicts various violence measures over a 4-

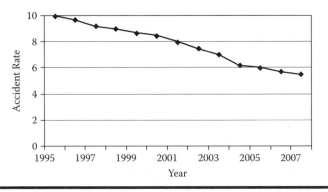

Figure 6.2 A descriptive performance measurement plot illustrating an overall decrease in accident rate over time.

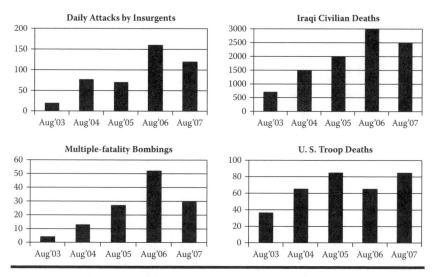

Figure 6.3   A family of violence-related descriptive performance measures associated with the Iraqi war. Note yearly measures from only the month of August are used in the various plots.

year period in the ongoing conflict in Iraq. Using only figures for the month of August from 2003 to 2007, you can clearly observe that violence has steadily escalated with an observed slight to moderate drop in August 2007.

An even more insightful set of descriptive measures relating to the Iraqi conflict is illustrated in Figure 6.4. Instead of using normal frequency plots as in Figure 6.3, in this example I have plotted violence-related data via the use of cumulative frequency graphs. Examining Figure 6.4, you can clearly discern that the numbers of foreign national kidnappings (Figure 6.4(a)) and U.S. military car bomb–related fatalities (Figure 6.4(b)) are in a (one can only hope!) late mature life cycle growth stage, as illustrated by well-developed S-shaped curve forms. Conversely, plots show that U.S. military improvised explosive device–related fatalities (Figure 6.4(c)) and estimated number of Iraqi civilian fatalities (Figure 6.4(d)) do not appear to have reached this same late mature life cycle stage growth form.

It is interesting to note both the similarities and differences among the graphs plotted in Figure 6.4. As depicted, Figures 6.4(a) and (b) show very different curve forms when compared to Figures 6.4(c) and (d). Often, unique and differing individual life cycle stages are associated with the same phenomenon. As illustrated in Figure 6.4 and depending on the individual circumstances, cumulative frequency plots often provide more descriptive and predictive value and visual insight than do more commonly used normal frequency plots.

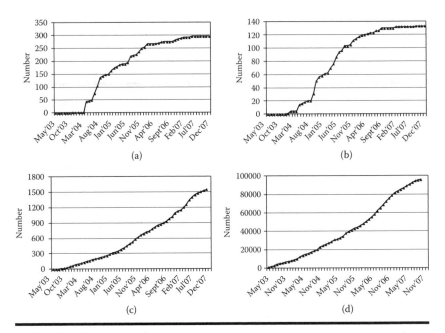

Figure 6.4 Violence-related cumulative frequency graphs from the Iraqi conflict. Graphical plots depict the cumulative number of foreign nationals kidnapped (a), U.S. military car bomb–related fatalities (b), U.S. military improvised explosive device–related fatalities (c), and estimated Iraqi civilian fatalities (d).

In another descriptive measure example, Figure 6.5 displays opium production measured in metric tons from the two main opium-producing countries of the world, Afghanistan and Myanmar. Note how Figure 6.5 depicts two very different trends for the two countries. For Myanmar, we observe an overall decreasing trend, one that may suggest a relatively successful anti-drug campaign. Conversely, for Afghanistan, the overall trend is one of increasing production, with the observed exception in 2001, when the ruling Taliban essentially wiped out opium production in the country. By analogy, one can hypothesize a failed drug enforcement and eradication policy in Afghanistan.

Figures 6.2 through 6.5 each measure or describe a specific outcome (or outcomes) over a defined time period. Armed with such historical- or temporal-based knowledge, the viewer can sometimes predict or at least postulate potential future trends. Yet extreme caution must always be exercised in such forward trending or predictive straight-line efforts. Remember from previous chapters that in performance speak, what goes up (or down) eventually flattens out!

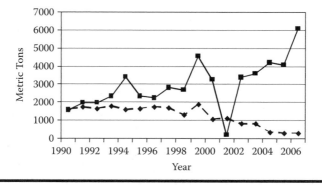

Figure 6.5 Potential opium production measured in metric tons from the countries of Afghanistan (solid line) and Myanmar (dashed line). Although starting out with essentially the same production figures, note the difference in overall trends for the two countries as a function of time.

Predictive Measures

Predictive measures are used to infer the future or extrapolate from one measure to another. They attempt to predict what *may* happen but to date has not happened. Such predictive "what may happen" interpretations are often predicated or based on "what has already happened" interpretations. Accordingly, predictive measures are also sometimes termed *leading indicators*, suggesting that they represent forward-looking types of measures.

In truth and despite much rhetoric to the contrary, many predictive measures are quite difficult to develop and almost always require some type of extrapolation or interpretation. Yet the more we know about life cycle growth, logistic functions, and how performance does and does not improve, the more predictive performance measures become.

Figure 6.6 plots two descriptive performance curves that represent different stages of logistic growth. Knowing essentially nothing about the graphs or what they represent, you can still make some tentative predictions about future growth based only on observed curve form. Accordingly, you could state that the graph on the left in Figure 6.6 appears to still be in an inflationary growth period and may continue at its current rate into the foreseeable future. Yet you could also express a certain caution, knowing that rapid growth eventually transitions to slowed growth, and then to no growth.

In contrast, the graph on the right in Figure 6.6 is in a decidedly deflationary and slowed growth mode. This observed slowed growth mode will, in time, most likely transition into a no-growth state unless some type of renewed growth innovation takes place.

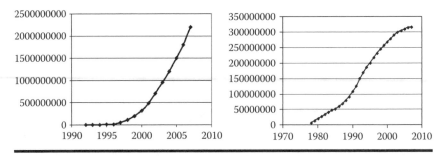

Figure 6.6 **Two very different S-curve plots resulting from differing stages in life cycle growth. The curve on the left is in a fairly immature, inflationary life cycle stage, whereas the one on the right is in a decidedly more mature and deflationary stage as evidenced by an almost complete S-shaped curve growth form.**

Often, when you juxtapose the plots of two descriptive measures in the same graph form, a great deal of predictive value emerges. This juxtaposition value was illustrated in Figure 6.1, where food production and population growth were plotted on the same graph form. In this instance, you see a strong negative correlation or relationship between one measure and another measure. When given a set or fixed amount of food, for example, as the population increases, the amount of available food will decrease.

Such observed correlations imply a mutual relationship or linkage between two or more variables. If you know that two variables are correlated and you measure one of those variables, you can often predict the other. In statistical speak, *correlation* is a measure of the relation between two or more variables.

A statistical correlation is expressed as a *coefficient.* Correlation coefficients can range from –1.00 to +1.00. A correlation coefficient value of –1.00 represents a perfect *negative correlation.* In a negative correlation, the relationship between two variables is such that as one variable's value tends to increase (population), the other variable's value tends to decrease (food).

Conversely, the value of +1.00 represents a perfect *positive correlation* coefficient. In a positive correlation, the relationship between two variables is such that as one variable's value tends to increase, the other variable's value also tends to increase. As you may have expected, a correlation coefficient of 0.00 represents a complete lack of correlation.

Let us examine two correlation examples, one where we note a very strong positive correlation and another illustrating a rather weak correlation. In the world of sports, there are some basic rules governed by physics that apparently explain why high-performing distance runners and cyclists look different from equally high-performing swimmers and rowers. These rules of physics dictate that competitive distance cycling and running favor small people, whereas rowing and swimming apparently favor people who are big. Most elite male marathoners, especially those who come from Kenya, Ethiopia, and other similar countries, for example, are between 5 foot 7 inches and 5 foot 11 inches tall and weigh between 120 and 140 pounds. Conversely, great male swimmers are often well over 6 feet tall and muscular. From such data we can generalize that there is a strong positive correlation between a larger size and swimming and rowing, and between a smaller size and distance running and cycling.

Gina Kolata, in a September 27, 2007, article appearing in the *New York Times*, does an excellent job explaining these observed body size–to–performance outcome correlations. She reports that when Dr. Neils H. Secher, an anesthesiologist, exercise researcher, and rower at the University of Copenhagen attempted to predict how fast competitive rowers could row based only on their size and weight of their boats, he was accurate to within 1 percent—he found an almost perfect positive correlation between rower size and boat weight and speed. In this particular instance, the reason why size is so important is because bigger rowers have bigger muscles, which translates positively into essentially having a bigger and more powerful motor in the boat.

In turn, distance sports like running and cycling favor smaller motors. Kolata notes that in distance running, even though tall people have longer stride lengths, stride length, as it turns out, does not determine speed. How we humans run is by lifting our bodies off the ground with each step and propelling ourselves forward. The more we weigh, however, the harder we have to work to lift our bodies off the ground. With increasing distance, we thus have to work harder and harder, and as a result, we become slower and slower.

This observation of why bigger is not necessarily better in this case explains why the best distance runners are usually small, light, and have slim legs. Small runners simply do not have to lift as heavy a load with each step as do larger runners. Thus, in this particular case, there is a positive correlation between small and lightweight bodies and distance-running performance.

It is important to note that in the real world there are always exceptions to such observations; some great distance runners are tall and some elite swimmers short. For example, American marathon runners often defy this small and light norm witnessed in other countries. That is why correlations are almost never perfect +1.00s and −1.00s. The closer we come to these ideal numbers, however, the greater their predictive value.

Let us briefly examine an example where you can observe a weak correlation between two entities. Chapter 1 noted a weak correlation or relationship between payroll size and winning the World Series. But what about payroll size and regular season wins? Figure 6.7 plots payroll size versus team wins for the 2007 regular Major League Baseball season. Calculating a correlation for the

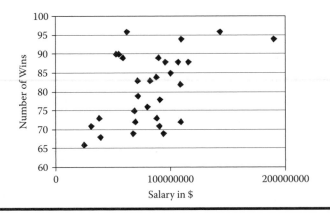

Figure 6.7 A graphical plot of Major League Baseball team salaries versus total team wins for the 2007 regular baseball season. As noted, the correlation coefficient between team wins and team salaries for this plot is +0.37.

plotted data gives a coefficient of +0.37, which is not an exceptionally strong correlation. Although in 2007, high-priced teams like the Boston Red Sox and the New York Yankees certainly won lots of games, so did lower-priced teams like the Cleveland Indians, Colorado Rockies, and Arizona Diamondbacks.

Referring to Figure 5.7, which is the exact same plot as Figure 6.7, except for the 2002 season, the correlation coefficient is essentially the same, +0.35. Apparently money is not quite the magical oomph factor that many baseball owners portend it to be.

You may wonder about the correlation between the number of wins and regular season attendance. Do winning teams attract more paying fans? Although there are many factors that affect regular season attendance other than team wins (such as associated team area population size and stadium seating capacity), you could run a correlation for the 2007 season and see what you discover. In doing so, you would observe a moderate correlation between number of wins and attendance, with a calculated correlation coefficient of +0.52. As illustrated, using one measure to predict another measure often provides a number of interesting insights, sometimes validating a strongly held assumption and at other times invalidating it.

Prescriptive Measures

Prescriptive measures are useful in diagnosing and sometimes improving performance-related problems. Ideally, prescriptive measures answer the question of what can (and can't) be done to improve performance.

Referring back to Figure 6.1 and based on your previously accrued knowledge of logistic growth, the plotted graph forms not only help you understand what has, is, and may happen (that is, that population growth may exceed food production), but also gives you some possible insights into how you may prevent the unwanted "what may happen" prediction by slowing population growth. As such, Figure 6.1 not only graphically describes and predicts what is and may happen, but also helps you diagnose and prescribe some corrective and, in this case, preventive actions.

In many instances, prescriptive measures represent in-process, means, or x types of measures. For example, the time it takes to run the 100-meter dash is an outcome (or Y-type) measure. Conversely, the number of steps a runner takes per second is a means (or x-type) measure. In turn, the number of steps taken per second, along with the stride or length of each step, ultimately contributes to the time it takes to run the 100-meter dash. In this example concerning sprint-type races, stride length does matter. Measuring and knowing such 'means' information can often help you better diagnose specific performance problems at ever-increasing levels of detail.

Ideally, the plot of a single measure represents a combined descriptive, predictive, and prescriptive measure. Although such plots are possible, they often require a certain requisite understanding and associated interpretation. Yet the greater your performance knowledge base, the greater the amount of information that may be abstracted from such measures.

For example, Figure 6.8 represents a slightly different plot in the decrease of accidents over time from that originally plotted in Figure 6.2. Given only the information displayed in Figure 6.8, how might you interpret the plotted data?

First, you might observe that although accident frequency has decreased over time, improvement efforts have currently stalled, reaching a pronounced asymptote as represented by the flat, bottom-right portion of the curve. Understanding the significance of such observed asymptotes, you should by now realize that merely doing more of the same (continuing to add even more safety-related procedures and rules) will likely result in little, if any, additional result. Current total performance capacity (TPC) in Figure 6.8 appears to be essentially tapped out. Based on the understanding gained in Chapter 4 about restarting the performance improvement process anew via innovation, you would most likely need to implement something new if you are to truly make any type of significant improvement in reducing accident rate.

In many instances, however, you cannot use a single graphical plot as that depicted in Figure 6.1 or 6.8 to capture and display all three measurement types. For example, Figure 6.9 graphs the time it takes for various individuals to complete an obstacle course. The course is comprised of nine distinct stages. At each

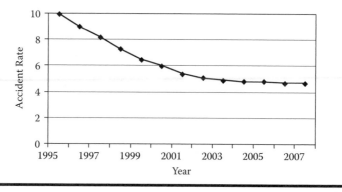

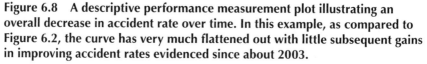

Figure 6.8 **A descriptive performance measurement plot illustrating an overall decrease in accident rate over time. In this example, as compared to Figure 6.2, the curve has very much flattened out with little subsequent gains in improving accident rates evidenced since about 2003.**

stage, individuals must perform a specific physical activity that tests strength, accuracy, or endurance.

Note that the frequency distribution depicted in Figure 6.9 resembles a fairly well-developed normal curve. Based on the distribution displayed in Figure 6.9, and knowing nothing else about the subject population, you can predict that most people who attempt the obstacle course will complete it in 300 to 480 seconds (given that they resemble the subject population). As such, Figure 6.9 has both descriptive value and some predictive value. However, it has little specific predictive value for where a given individual would likely fall along the plotted time distribution. In some instances, you may wish to predict how particular individuals will perform prior to their attempting the obstacle course.

Let us assume that 2 weeks prior to individuals attempting the obstacle course, they must first complete the 1-mile run and 40-yard dash. Armed with these previously collected times, you can construct a simple correlation matrix between 1-mile and 40-yard dash times and subsequent obstacle course times. We may find, for example, a fairly strong correlation (+0.83) between participants' 1-mile run times and their obstacle course times. Conversely, times in the 40-yard dash have a very low correlation coefficient (+0.11) or predictive value with obstacle course times.

From such analyses, you can conclude that 1-mile run times have fairly high value in predicting subsequent obstacle course times, whereas the 40-yard dash has low predictive value. If, for example, an individual's 1-mile run time is fairly slow, that individual will, in all probability, plot on the right side of the graph depicted in Figure 6.9 when attempting the obstacle course.

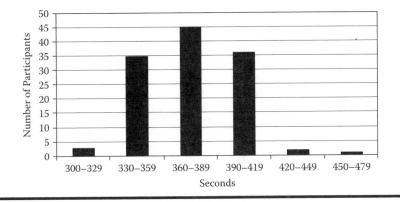

Figure 6.9   A frequency distribution of the time required to successfully complete a hypothetical obstacle course. Note that the bulk of times cluster between 330 and 420 seconds.

For individual diagnostic purposes, however, you would most likely want to continue to zoom in with your measures a bit more. Figure 6.10 plots overall average and individual participant times for each stage of the obstacle course. Note in Figure 6.10(a) that one participant seems to mimic average times fairly well except for Stage 5, where his time is considerably above average. In Figure 6.10(b), you see a similar plot for another individual, except that, in this case, his time increases above the average significantly at Stage 8. Understanding the specifics of what is entailed in the two stages and why the individuals are having such observed difficulties could, in turn, possibly help you prescribe a given improvement solution.

As illustrated and with careful forethought, much can be learned from capturing and displaying differing performance metrics. Unfortunately and all too often, organizations collect, plot, and display performance metric scorecards and dashboards without fully understanding what such measures do and do not tell us about performance. Although collecting and displaying performance metrics are important, metrics *plus* the corresponding interpretive knowledge are even more important. To fully maximize the benefit of any performance measurement effort, it is critical to understand what measures can and cannot tell us about performance.

Before implementing any performance measurement effort, however, we must first select what to measure. In other words, before we determine *how to measure* something we must first determine *what to measure*. As described in the following section, this "what to measure" selection process should be driven and preceded by the development of a domain-specific performance model. Models of performance should thus determine measures of performance.

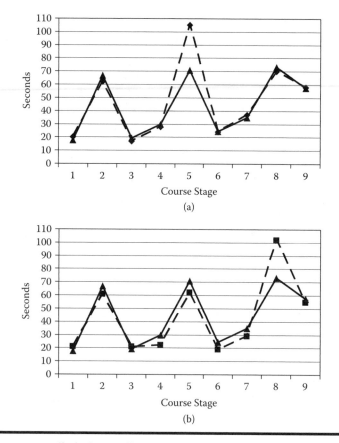

Figure 6.10 Detailed plots at the individual stage level for the described obstacle course as measured in seconds. Note the plots show both average (solid line) and individual participant (dashed line) times. As illustrated, the individual participant in (a) is experiencing considerable difficulty with Stage 5 when compared to the average. Conversely, the participant in (b) is having trouble completing Stage 8 in a timely manner.

Models of Performance Should Drive Measures of Performance

While observing differing approaches to implementing performance measurement systems in varying organizations, I have reached the conclusion that most organizations struggle not so much with the actual mechanics or technology of performance measurement, but rather with the more theoretical aspects of performance measurement. They often experience problems in identifying *what* to measure, the specific *units* of measure to use, and as noted, how to correctly *interpret* measures once they have been collected and displayed. As such, we continue our discussion of measuring performance by first tackling the "what to measure" question.

When I was researching my third book, entitled *The Basics of Performance Measurement*, I had the fortunate opportunity to talk to a number of organizations about their respective performance measurement systems. I quickly learned to ask two leading questions: (1) What measures do you collect? (2) Of those collected measures, which ones do you actually use? In most instances, I found that although the interviewed organizations were collecting a number of measures, they were actually using only a very small subset of that collected total. But those few measures that they were using proved invaluable for managing, assessing, and improving the performance of their respective organizations.

This discovery seems to represent both good and bad news. Although measuring performance certainly adds value, not all measures offer the same or equal amount of value. In many instances, organizations are exerting more resources in collecting and plotting performance-related measures than they are realizing actual value from those measures.

When inquiring further as to how they initially identified what measures to collect, most organizations reported that they simply brainstormed a possible list of performance measures and that is what they ended up collecting. In such instances there was no systematic identification process used to identify a preferred set of performance measures. It was basically a hit-and-miss proposition! Consequently, some measures were of incredible value (such as the hits), whereas others added little or no value at all, representing little more than Mark Twain's cursed statistics.

It is suggested that a better approach to determining the "what to measure" question is to first start with a performance model. Referring to Chapter 5, I noted that a model is simply an abstraction of the real world. Models, in turn, are often built via the process of decomposition. As illustrated in Figure 6.11, decomposition results in a hierarchical model composed of upper-level component objects, mid-level sub-objects, and lower-level elements and even sub-elements.

From a performance perspective, identified objects are those critical few oomph factors that drive performance outcomes. That is, objects represent critical x's that drive some performance outcome Y. Thus, by creating a performance model, you have not only identified outcome Y and critical object set x, but by virtue of association, you have also identified what to measure. Thus, the answer to the "what to measure" question is that you measure the previously identified set of model objects.

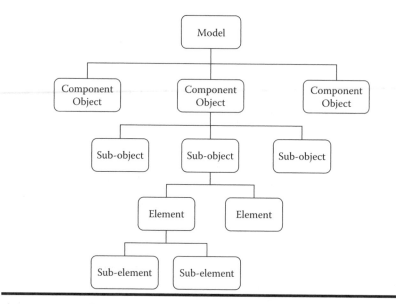

Figure 6.11   As illustrated once again, performance models can be decomposed into various types of objects. When answering the "what to measure" question, one should always measure identified performance objects.

Although you may not know exactly how to measure those objects, what units of measurement to use, or even how far down the hierarchy you should measure, the "what to measure" question is straightforward: you measure objects.

Accordingly, if human development is driven by a long and healthy life, knowledge, and a decent standard of living, you measure a long and healthy life, knowledge, and a decent standard of living. In turn, if you decompose a long and healthy life (as measured by life expectancy) into infant, adolescent, and maternal mortality, you measure infant, adolescent, and maternal mortality.

Or if you know that container ship profitability is driven by the time cargo-filled vessels are under way minus the time vessels are in port, you measure the time cargo-filled vessels are under way minus the time vessels are in port. Or if offensive efficiency in basketball is primarily a function of field goal attempts made, free throw attempts made, turnovers, and offensive rebounds, you measure field goal attempts made, free throw attempts made, turnovers, and offensive rebounds.

The bottom line is that you measure those key factors or objects that drive performance, using your previously developed performance model to identify those measures. Models of performance then, especially domain-specific models, should always determine measures of performance.

Often, as you delve lower in your hierarchical-based performance model, upper-level descriptive measures transform into lower-level diagnostic or prescriptive measures. For example, you may find that Country Z has only a moderate Human Development Index. This moderate HDI figure for Country Z is primarily caused by a lower-than-expected life expectancy rate. Upon closer examination, you find that lower-than-expected life expectancy is adversely affected by high adolescent mortality numbers. If you further measure the number of adolescents inoculated per 100,000 children (an important x factor affecting adolescent mortality), you may discover relatively low inoculation numbers. Such a discovery, in turn, suggests a possible cause for the moderate HDI figure and a prescribed action: the need to more widely inoculate susceptible adolescents.

Although performance models and embedded object sets tell you what drives a particular phenomenon (such as human development), it is the corresponding measures of those objects that often tell you how that phenomenon is actually performing. This is why performance models and performance measures must be closely linked. Although a well-constructed performance model helps to answer the "What drives performance?" question, a corresponding set of related measures answers the "How is it performing?" question. Such measures can further answer the "What is wrong?" and "What may happen next?" questions as well.

Once you develop a comprehensive and domain-specific performance model, the "What do we measure?" question is easily answered. You simply measure your identified object set (those factors that critically drive performance). Yet an often overlooked aspect of this need is identifying the correct unit of measure, a topic I explore more fully in the following section.

Units of Measurement

The "what to measure" question is answered by the $Y = f(x)$ performance model. The short answer is that you measure both the outcome Y and the performance factor set x. An often overlooked second step in developing any performance measurement system, however, is identifying the appropriate *unit of measure*, especially for your x factors.

Imagine, for example, that you run a large, federally funded training center, one that offers a variety of training courses. Delivery costs (the amount of money that must be spent to put on a particular course) vary considerably. For example, one course, labeled Course A, costs $200,000 to deliver. Another course, Course B, costs $90,000, and a third course, Course C, costs $50,000. Which course costs the most to deliver?

If you are looking only at total costs, the answer is obvious: Course A costs more than Course B, which in turn costs more than Course C. Yet further examination reveals that the three courses are very different in both course length and the number of attending students.

Course A lasts 6 weeks and consists of sixteen students. Course B is a week-long course and has twenty attending students. Finally, Course C is only 2 days in length, but enrolls fifty students. Now which course costs the most?

If you purposely ignore course length, you could calculate a per student cost. Take total course cost and divide that figure by the number of students enrolled in the course. This approach would indicate that per student costs for the three courses are as follows:

■ Course A: $12,500 per student ($200,000 ÷ 16)
■ Course B: $4,500 per student ($90,000 ÷ 20)
■ Course C: $1,000 per student ($50,000 ÷ 50)

Yet this approach ignores the length of each course. Accordingly, a more accurate per unit measure is the actual cost per student day, determined by dividing student cost by course length as measured in days. As such, the cost differential among the three courses as determined by the cost of an individual student training day is as follows:

■ Course A: $417 per training day ($12,500 ÷ 30 days)
■ Course B: $900 per training day ($4,500 ÷ 5 days)
■ Course C: $500 per training day ($1,000 ÷ 2 days)

Note that when you select total cost, Course A is more than twice as expensive as Course B. Yet when you select the unit measure "cost per student training day," the exact reverse is true, with Course B now being more than twice as expensive as Course A. By selecting an appropriate unit of measure, you can often learn a great deal of information about a particular performance metric and associated x factor.

Referring to Chapter 5, it was noted that basketball wins are solely a function of offensive and defensive efficiency, as determined by what you do when your team possesses the ball (offensive efficiency) and what you do when the other team possesses the ball (defensive efficiency). It was further noted that offensive efficiency is measured by points scored per possession employed, while defensive efficiency is measured by points allowed per possession acquired. You may wonder why I elect to use per possession and not per game as the basic unit of measure.

Berri, Schmidt, and Brook do an excellent job explaining the importance of a possession in their book *The Wages of Wins*. Their quote from John Hollinger (2002) is especially insightful. According to Hollinger:

> Possessions are the basic currency of basketball. No matter what the team does with the ball—score, turns the ball over, or misses a shot—the other team gets it back when they are done. The objective of basketball is to score more points than the other team: put that in terms of possessions, and the goal is to score as many points per possession as possible while limiting the opponent to as few points per possession as possible.

Additionally, in any given basketball game, the number of possessions essentially equals out. Each team basically has the same number of possessions *within* a game. Conversely, the number of possessions *among* games can vary widely depending on the pace of the game. One only has to watch a Phoenix Suns' game with and without superstar Steve Nash playing to understand this differential pace observation.

Accordingly, some professional basketball teams may rank quite high in points scored per possession employed, but lower in points scored per game. Yet as described by Hollinger, the unit of measure of greatest importance and value is not what happens on a per game basis, but rather what happens on a per possession basis. As such, selecting the right unit of measure for any performance metric is of critical importance.

Selecting appropriate units of measure not only helps us better describe performance, but also assists us in better diagnosing performance problems. For example, the total time it takes to run the 100-meter dash is a good example of an outcome or Y measure. Yet from a diagnostic point of view, it tells you little except that one runner is faster or slower than another runner. You may wish on occasion to know why one runner is faster or slower than another runner. In this case, stride frequency as measured by steps per second may be a better measure. Most elite female sprinters, for example, take approximately 4.6 steps per second. Slower numbers indicate that a sprinter is simply not getting her feet back off the ground fast enough with each step.

Additionally, even the best sprinters of the world slow down in the last 10 to 15 meters of a 100-meter sprint. Dividing the total time to run the 100-meter dash into times based on 10- or 15-meter increments can determine just how much a sprinter is actually slowing down in the final segment of a race. It can also determine how long it takes a sprinter to reach top speed at the start of a race.

Interpreting Measures of Performance

Selecting the right unit of measurement, especially for the critical x factors, is one key to better describing, predicting, and diagnosing performance. As is demonstrated in our SPOTC-related case study at the end of this chapter, careful consideration should always be given to selected units of performance measurement. In selecting the wrong unit of measurement (for example, points scored per game in basketball), you may unintentionally and mistakenly mask the truly important unit of measure (which is points scored per possession). Before demonstrating the importance of selecting the appropriate unit of measure, however, it may prove valuable to spend at least a bit of time discussing the importance of correctly *interpreting* measures of performance.

One's ability to understand, manage, and improve performance is predicated on the ability to successfully measure performance. Yet this statement is further based on the ability to derive meaningful information from such measures and associated graphical plots. This need, in turn, is a function of understanding how performance does and does not improve over time, the role of innovation, and the general precepts of life cycle and logistic growth.

Perhaps the greatest value in accruing such performance-based understandings is knowing what is normal or expected, what is not, and what may possibly be causing that "what is not." In other words, you are improving your ability to adequately explain both the expected and unexpected in terms of life cycle growth.

For example, you expect the frequency and magnitude of performance gains within a single lineage to decrease over time. Given sufficient time, these decreases in both magnitude and frequency result in a normal S-shaped performance curve form, as illustrated in numerous graphical plots throughout this book.

In turn, if you divide your resultant S-shaped curve into four time-based quartiles and calculate percent improvement within each quartile, you would expect to observe an overall decrease in performance improvement as a function of time. This temporal-related percentage decrease in performance gains, in turn, should result in a concave-upward-looking curve plot.

Figure 6.12 replots world water speed record progression for internal combustion engine–powered speed boats. Figure 6.13 divides that plot into quartiles and displays the percent increase in speed within each quartile. Note that as normally expected, percent increase in speed decreases as a function of time, resulting in the plotted curve displaying a characteristic concave-upward appearance. Also note that the greatest change or percent improvement in speed occurs in the first quartile, the second greatest change in the second quartile (albeit significantly much less than the first quartile), and so on.

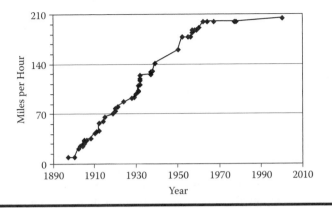

Figure 6.12 World water speed record progression for internal combustion engine, propeller-driven speedboats.

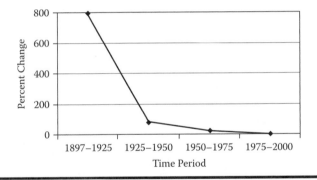

Figure 6.13 If the graph form depicted in Figure 6.12 is divided into four temporal-based quadrants and percent change within each quadrant is plotted, then, as illustrated, a concave-upward-looking curve results. Note that in such plots the biggest gains in performance as measured by change in percentage accrue between the first and second quadrants, with subsequent changes and associated performance gains decreasing markedly.

Figure 6.14 plots percent improvement by quartile for world land speed record progression for wheel-driven vehicles. Once again, you see essentially the same thing, an overall decrease in percent improvement as a function of time and a concave-upward-looking curve plot. Note, however, that both Figures 6.13 and 6.14 represent only a single, within-lineage curve plot. What happens if you attempt to mix lineages together in the same curve plot?

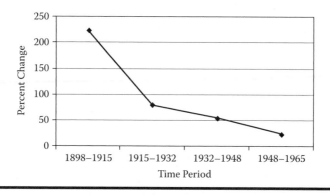

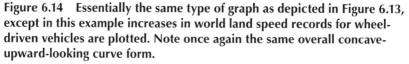

Figure 6.14 Essentially the same type of graph as depicted in Figure 6.13, except in this example increases in world land speed records for wheel-driven vehicles are plotted. Note once again the same overall concave-upward-looking curve form.

Figure 6.15 does just that for world land speed record progression. Note the resultant anomalous and significant bump in the third quartile. Your expected concave-upward-looking plot now looks decidedly different, doesn't it? The reason for this apparent anomaly is the role of innovation in restarting the improvement process anew via the introduction of thrust-based, vehicle-powered technologies. As illustrated in Figure 6.15, it is always important when interpreting graphical plots of varying performance measures to be able to explain both the expected and the unexpected, or why a given performance graph form does or does not follow expected norms. Let us examine this expected-versus-unexpected performance norm concept a bit more closely.

On Sunday July 29, 2007, and after 2,206 miles and 23 days of exhaustive effort, the best cyclists in the world pedaled down the Champs-Elysees to complete the Tour de France. Unfortunately, the prestigious 2007 race, like the earlier 2006 race when winner Floyd Landis tested positive for a banned performance-enhancing substance, was sullied by continued doping problems and allegations of doping. To indicate the magnitude of the problem in the 2007 race, three of the top riders, including the race leader and a pre-race favorite, and two competing teams were either kicked out of the Tour de France or dropped out voluntarily because of failed drug tests or suspicion of avoiding anti-doping officials. Indeed, throughout the 2007 Tour de France, there were probably as many—if not more—newspaper articles written about the doping problem as there were articles written about the actual race itself.

On that same Sunday in July 2007, baseball slugger Barry Bonds was one home run shy of tying Hank Aaron's 755 career home run record (in the following days, Bonds would go on to tie and then break Aaron's record). Yet like many

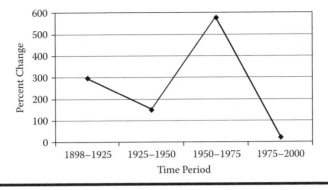

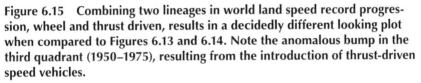

Figure 6.15 Combining two lineages in world land speed record progression, wheel and thrust driven, results in a decidedly different looking plot when compared to Figures 6.13 and 6.14. Note the anomalous bump in the third quadrant (1950–1975), resulting from the introduction of thrust-driven speed vehicles.

of the cyclists riding in the Tour de France that day, Bonds was surrounded by controversy and associated charges that he had previously used performance-enhancing steroids to unfairly assist him in his home run record pursuit. In fact, for much of the 2007 season, whenever he ventured outside of his home field in San Francisco, fans often booed him and held signs proclaiming that the great Hank Aaron didn't cheat.

Yet perhaps the crowning blow to the so-called steroid age came on Thursday, December 13, 2007, when former senate majority leader George Mitchell made public the results of a 20-month investigation into performance-enhancing drug usage in major league baseball. The 409-page report entitled *Report to the Commissioner of Baseball of an Independent Investigation into the Illegal Use of Steroids and Other Performance Enhancing Substances by Players in Major League Baseball,* quickly shortened to the Mitchell Report, implicated more than eighty former and current Major League Baseball players. Names published in the report included such greats as Barry Bonds, Roger Clemens, Andy Pettitte, and Miguel Tejada. The published list of abusers accounted for 8,502 home runs, 8 Cy Young winners (7 by Clemens and 1 by Eric Gagne), 15 MVP titles, and 37 World Series rings.

The next day's front-page headlines of *USA Today* called the report's disturbing accusations "A Collective Failure," with the sub-headline proclaiming "Some of Sport's Top Stars Implicated." President Bush even commented on the report, noting in a recorded speech that "steroids had sullied the game."

The lengthy report addresses a number of perplexing drug-related issues and accusations. Yet ironically, the Mitchell Report makes a basic, fundamental, and unaddressed assumption: that performance-enhancing substances, be they steroids or human growth hormone, actually enhance performance. The report, and most everyone else for that matter, simply assumes that such substances enhance athletic performance, giving illegal users an unfair competitive advantage over legal non-users. Yet how do we prove such allegations of performance enhancement? That is, do performance-enhancing drugs, in fact, actually enhance performance?

If you think of performance-enhancing substances as representing an innovation, albeit a decidedly illegal one, then should you observe corresponding anomalous spikes in performance records similar to that observed in Figure 6.15? The problem we face of course by asking this question is that we really do not know who did and didn't use such banned substances. Tragically, however, there is one exception to this "who really did and didn't" corundum, and that is the athletes representing the German Democratic Republic (GDR) government in the 1970s and 1980s.

In a scholarly article entitled "Hormonal Doping and Androgenization of Athletes: A Secret Program of the German Democratic Republic Government" that appeared in a 1997 special issue on doping in sports in the academic journal *Clinical Chemistry*, authors Werner Franke and Brigitte Berendock describe in detail the systematic use of performance-enhancing substances by the GDR government for improving athletic performance. Of particular interest here is the often unknown or ignorant use of such substances (commonly portrayed as only vitamins by coaches and trainers alike) by the women's swim team.

As illustrated in Table 6.1, between 1972 and 1988, GDR women swimmers dominated the swimming world, setting a combined total of 81 world records in the 100m and 200m breaststroke, backstroke, butterfly, and freestyle swimming events. Overall increase in performance for this time period in the eight events equaled 7.5 percent.

Yet also depicted in Table 6.1, over the same approximate time period and in the same eight events, the U.S. men's swim team set sixty-five records and accrued an overall increase in performance of 4.9 percent. With the likes of Mark Spitz leading the way, the United States was equally dominant. How then do we compare such similar results?

Remember in statistics that size really does matter. Accordingly, we must place the time interval of 1972 to 1988 in its proper perspective. Figure 6.16 divides percent improvement in men's swimming performance for the eight described Olympic events into four quartiles, much like what we did in earlier graphical representations. The four quartiles cover the approximate time periods prior to 1956, 1956–1972, 1972–1988 (our period of interest), and post-1988.

Table 6.1 Percent Change in Time and Number of Olympic Records Set by the German Democratic Republic Women's Swim Team and the U.S. Men's Swim Team between Approximately 1972 and 1988

Event (1972–1988)	Women % Change/No. GDR Records	Men % Change/No. U.S. Records
100m backstroke	7.3%/13	3.2%/8
100m breaststroke	7.7%/15	6.4%/12
100m butterfly	9.3%/9	3.4%/8
100m freestyle	6.4%/14	5.9%/13
200m backstroke	8.6%/9	3.8%/4
200m breaststroke	7.1%/7	6.9%/6
200m butterfly	7.8%/7	4.6%/6
200m freestyle	6.1%/7	4.9%/8
Avg % change/total records	7.5%/81	4.9%/65

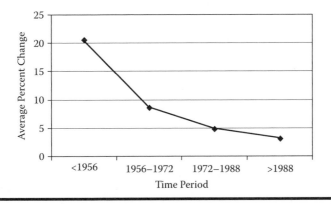

Figure 6.16 Average percent changes in overall speed (divided into four temporal-based quadrants) for men's Olympic swimming. Note plotted percentages include the men's 100m and 200m breaststroke, butterfly, backstroke, and freestyle swim events.

Note that Figure 6.16 displays the expected concave upward graph form, with a decrease in percentage recorded for each successive quartile. Although the plot illustrated in Figure 6.16 does not conclusively prove that performance-enhancing substances were not used, it certainly conforms to normal expectations concerning overall decreases in performance improvement as a function of time.

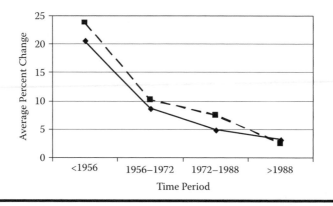

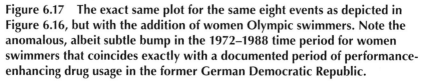

Figure 6.17   The exact same plot for the same eight events as depicted in Figure 6.16, but with the addition of women Olympic swimmers. Note the anomalous, albeit subtle bump in the 1972–1988 time period for women swimmers that coincides exactly with a documented period of performance-enhancing drug usage in the former German Democratic Republic.

Figure 6.17 represents the same plot, but this time percent improvements in women swimming are also added to each quartile. Note that we see a slight, and you might say unexpected, bump for the 1972 through 1988 time period, a period for which we have definitive and documented proof that GDR swimmers were using performance-enhancing substances. Given such knowledge of illegal doping activity within the GDR, it is certainly a bit suspicious that the observed and admittedly subtle bump in our plotted performance data occurs in the exact same time interval of interest.

We also know that such banned substances were given to GDR track-and-field athletes as well. For example, in 1988, GDR discus thrower Gabriele Reinsch set the world record in the women's discus event with a throw of 76.80 m. To date, the record still stands. As illustrated in Figure 6.18, you can plot improvement in performance for the women's discus throw via four more or less equal quartiles beginning with the first record set in 1923.

Note that the first three quartiles follow the expected overall decrease in performance gain as a function of time. Yet also note the unexpected blip in the fourth quartile. Here, you observe an uncharacteristic curve form in terms of how performance normally does and does not improve as a function of time associated with a documented doping period. From such admittedly brief and circumstantial evidence, one might conclude that performance-enhancing substances actually do enhance performance via the introduction of a new innovation.

The take-away message, however, is not about performance-enhancing substances or the systematic doping of young and often unsuspecting GDR female

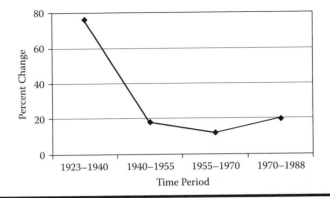

Figure 6.18 **A similar plot as illustrated in Figure 6.17 for the women's Olympic discus event. Note the upward trend for 1970–1988, the same documented doping period in the German Democratic Republic.**

athletes. Rather, it is about better understanding measures of performance and what such measures, admittedly often in very subtle ways, can and cannot tell us. It may be that the true DNA of performance, unlike its biological counterpart, is not depicted in strands of double helixes but rather in graphical plots of performance-related data. By better understanding the meaning of such plots, we may be able to better decipher and explain the expected from the unexpected, or the very essence of performance.

SPOTC Measures of Performance

In Chapter 5, we developed a SPOTC-specific performance model composed of three critical component objects: speed of movement, accuracy, and cognition for the Security Protection Officer Training Competition. We can now develop performance metrics to successfully measure each component object and associated sub-objects and elements, paying particular attention to developing prescriptive- or diagnostic-type measures. As will be illustrated in Chapter 7, prescriptive measures are particularly valuable in trying to diagnose and improve a particular performance-related problem.

To illustrate such needed performance measurement development efforts, we first develop measures for accuracy and speed of movement for the individual events. Next, we will develop cognition-related measures for the team competition.

For ease of illustration, I have greatly fictionalized and simplified the various courses of fire comprising SPOTC. In the depicted fictional scenario, the individual competition is now comprised of five events, or five courses of fire, labeled CF-1 through CF-5. CF-1 and CF-2 are rifle-only courses, CF-3 and CF-4 are pistol-only courses, and CF-5 is a rifle-pistol combined course.

Each course of fire is further comprised of the same three stages labeled S1, S2, and S3, respectively. Stage 1 (S1) has fixed or stationary targets and requires the participant to only fire from a single position. Stage 2 (S2) is also a single position of fire-only stage, but consists of moving targets that are fixed to a wheel that begins to rotate once the first target is hit. Stage 3 (S3) is comprised of fixed targets but has multiple firing positions (e.g., standing, kneeling, etc.). Remember that targets only have to be hit to receive a successful score. The exact location of the hit on the target is not scored or graded.

Let us begin by first developing performance metrics to measure accuracy. Because targets only have to be hit, I use rounds expended per target (REPT) as the basic unit of measure at the accuracy component object level. Accordingly, if someone fires ten rounds or bullets and hits ten targets, REPT is 1.0, representing the idealized or perfect figure. Conversely, if someone fires fifteen rounds and hits ten targets, REPT is 1.5.

Finally, let us plot accuracy as measured by REPT for four participants, labeled A–D, respectively. Figure 6.19 plots REPT for each course of fire (CF-1 through CF-5) involving our four participants (A through D). From Figure 6.19, we can clearly see that participant A is the best shot across all five courses of fire.

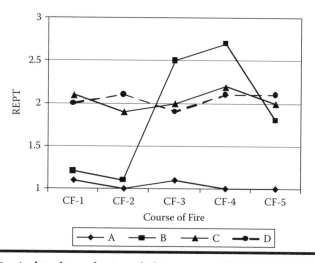

Figure 6.19 A plot of rounds expended per target (REPT) for five hypothetical courses of fire for four participants labeled A, B, C, and D. Note that whereas participants A, C, and D have fairly consistent REPT scores, the performance of participant B varies widely depending on the specific course of fire.

Conversely, participant B does well on CF-1 and CF-2, but poorly on CF-3 and CF-4 and only mediocre on CF-5. Remembering that CF-1 and CF-2 are rifle-only courses, CF-3 and CF-4 are pistol-only courses, and CF-5 is a rifle-pistol combined course, participant B is clearly a better rifle than pistol marksman.

Finally, note that participants C and D turn in only mediocre scores across all five courses of fire. Yet Figure 6.19 provides little "why" information regarding participant C's and D's performances. It appears that, in this case, we need better diagnostic information as represented by more detailed levels of performance measurement.

Remember that in Chapter 5, I decomposed the component object accuracy into sub-objects rifle and pistol, but elected not to decompose these individual sub-objects further. Recognizing that greater granularity is now needed, I can further decompose the sub-objects into the elements target type and firing position. Target type is further decomposed into the sub-elements stationary and moving. Additionally, firing position is decomposed into single and multiple.

With this further decomposition effort completed, we can now create graphs that plot REPT at the individual stage level for each course of fire for each participant. First examine participant C's newly created plots. Note in Figure 6.20 that participant C consistently has problems for each course of fire at Stage 2 irrespective of weapon type. Remembering that Stage 2 consists of a moving target, we can now identify participant C's primary problem: he is a poor shot at a moving target.

We can also plot participant D's performance in much the same manner as illustrated in Figure 6.21. Here we see consistent problems at Stage 3 for each course of fire. In this case, Stage 3 requires participants to assume multiple fir-

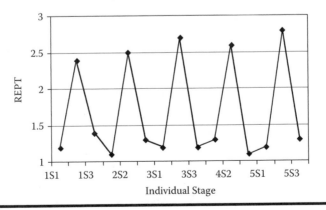

Figure 6.20 A plot of participant C at the individual stage level for each course of fire. As illustrated, participant C's accuracy decreases markedly at Stage 2 for each course of fire.

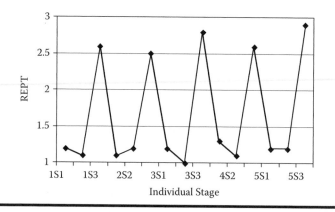

Figure 6.21 A plot of participant D at the individual stage level for each course of fire. As illustrated, participant D's accuracy decreases markedly at Stage 3 for each course of fire. Compare Figure 6.21 with Figure 6.20.

ing positions in rapid succession. As depicted in Figure 6.21, this requirement proves problematic for participant D.

Although we could certainly decompose the component object accuracy further, there appears little need. As illustrated, the developed model and associated performance measures seem adequate for describing and diagnosing performance outcomes as measured by average rounds expended per target at both the course of fire (in Figure 6.19) and individual stage levels (in Figures 6.20 and 6.21).

Continuing on, in Chapter 5 the component object speed of movement was further decomposed into sub-objects intrastage movement and interstage movement. In measuring speed, time is often a useful unit of measure and will be adopted here. In this example involving speed of movement, we will concentrate our efforts on measuring only interstage movement.

The sub-object interstage movement is affected by the element's distance and obstacles. Remember that, during SPOTC competition, various types of obstacles are often positioned between stages, thus requiring participants to go over, under, or through an obstacle before arriving at the next stage. To simplify matters, we can assume that distances between stages are essentially the same. Accordingly, the only real differentiating variable that we have to deal with in interstage movement is type of object.

For each course of fire, we can take three related interstage movement measures: the time it takes to go from the starting line to Stage 1 (ending with the first round being fired); the time it takes to go from Stage 2 to Stage 3 (beginning with the last round being fired at Stage 1 and ending with the first round being fired at Stage 2); and the time it takes to go from Stage 2 to Stage 3 (beginning with the last round being fired at Stage 2 and ending with the first round being fired at Stage 3).

Figure 6.22 plots interstage movement times for participant A. Note that, overall, such speed-related times are fairly consistent except in two instances (Stage 2 to 3 movement in CF-1, and Stage 2 to 3 movement in CF-4). A quick check indicates that the same type of crawl-through-a-culvert obstacle is present at both interstage sites. Participant A is having difficulty with a specific crawl-through obstacle.

As illustrated in the previous two examples, both accuracy and speed of movement are directly observable and measurable. Conversely, the third critical component object (cognition) proves a bit more problematic from a direct observation standpoint. Because cognition represents mental processing and resultant decision making, it is impossible to directly ascertain or observe what is going on in someone's head. This highlights that need for related measures that reflect cognitive performance (for example, good or bad decision making) and that can be directly observed and recorded or measured.

SPOTC consists primarily of people shooting, running, and shouting. Who is doing most of the shouting besides the audience is the captain of each team during the team competition events; remember that SPOTC is divided into both individual and team events, including one super-team event. What the captain is actually shouting are commands at critical points in the evolution of a team event. That is, Command 1 should be shouted at Time T1 in the team event competition, Command 2 at Time T2, and so forth. Fortunately, those shouted commands can be directly observed or heard.

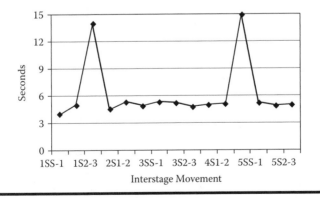

Figure 6.22   A plot of participant A's times as measured in seconds for interstage movement. Note times are fairly consistent except when moving from Stage 2 to Stage 3 in the first and fourth courses of fire (1S2-3 and 4S2-3).

People who study and measure team cognition label such overt actions (such as shouted commands) *cognitive markers*. Based on this cognitive marker concept, one can collect information on whether and when shouted commands occur during a SPOTC team event.

Table 6.2 records the presence or absence of cognitive markers for four captains competing in a single team event. In this example, present/absent recordings are made at ten differing time intervals labeled T1–T10 for four captains in the event. Note that Captain C has the highest successful cognitive marker rating (10 out of 10), whereas Captain A has the lowest rating (only 6 out of 10). If you further observe that Team C won the event and Team A came in last, you may have some valuable diagnostic evidence in helping explain potential differences in team performance.

As illustrated by our SPOTC example, performance *measures* should always be driven by performance *models*. In some instances, you may find that your performance model and associated measures are insufficient to provide the needed diagnostic and prescriptive information required to effectively improve performance. In such instances, additional model decomposition and associated measure development efforts are required. In Chapter 7, I will examine how the developed SPOTC-specific measures of performance can, in turn, be translated into specific performance improvement actions.

Table 6.2 A Performance Measure for Cognition Using the Concept of Cognitive Markers, as Measured by Correctly and Timely Shouted Commands

Time Interval	Captain A	Captain B	Captain C	Captain D
T1	X	X	X	X
T2		X	X	X
T3	X	X	X	X
T4			X	
T5	X	X	X	X
T6	X	X	X	X
T7	X	X	X	X
T8			X	X
T9		X	X	X
T10	X	X	X	X
Total	**6**	**8**	**10**	**9**

Summary

Measurement involves ascertaining the size, amount, or degree of something. Performance measurement attempts to measure or ascertain either the ends or outcomes of performance (value Y), and the means (x factors) that affect such outcomes. There are three basic types of performance measures: descriptive, predictive, and prescriptive measures. Note that in some instances and depending on how a measure is graphically displayed, the same measure may serve all three functions.

A descriptive measure describes what is happening or has happened. Such measures commonly depict a specific outcome and are often used to trend a particular phenomenon over time from a historical perspective. Predictive measures are used to infer the future. They attempt to predict what may happen but to date has not happened. Finally, prescriptive measures are useful in diagnosing and sometimes improving performance-related problems. Ideally, prescriptive measures answer the question of what we can (and can't) do to improve performance.

Performance models should drive selected performance measures. What should be measured are model-based objects that represent important performance oomph factors. Just as performance models via continued decomposition provide greater in-depth granularity, associated performance measurement systems via the same parallel decomposition process yield greater diagnostic and prescriptive resolution.

In many instances, what is needed is not the collection of ever more performance measurement data. Rather, what is actually needed is better processing, interpretation, and resultant understanding of already collected performance-related data.

Chapter 7

Improving Performance

In the spring of 1994, I taught a one-day business process reengineering workshop at a conference that was being held in San Francisco. Placing the experience in its best context, one could say that it proved a bit challenging. A more apt and honest assessment is that it turned out to be an unmitigated disaster!

I thought I came well prepared. I had my recently developed and previously published seven-step process improvement method for the how-to-do-it part of the workshop. I also brought along a series of case studies showcasing the effectiveness of my developed methodology. In my collection of real-world examples, including a performance gain in cycle time of some 70 percent in one instance, I just knew that I had the right mix of crowd pleasers. What more, I naively thought, could attending participants want or desire?

As it turned out, what they wanted were examples of real revolutions in performance improvement. Not my offered paltry gains in the tens of percent, but quantum, and I might add single, revolutionary leaps in the 100s to 1,000s of percent. Even after all these many years, I still vividly remember one particularly stinging critique comment that stated, "Dr. Harbour simply doesn't understand the difference between evolution and revolution. He's still a performance improvement Neanderthal. All in all, a very disappointing performance."

The passage of time has somewhat assuaged the wounds suffered from that admittedly painful and embarrassing experience. And I hope the previous chapters have also demonstrated that although revolutions in performance certainly do occur, gains spawned by those revolutions normally accrue one small increment at a time and rarely at the magnitude so lavishly and enthusiastically promised.

As illustrated by my own unsavory experience, a significant challenge in any performance improvement endeavor is setting and managing realistic expectations of both the improver and receiving customer alike. Yet, in retrospect, there were some things that I could have probably done better as well those many years ago.

During the workshop, I focused solely on methodology, failing to discuss other key factors that can also critically affect any performance improvement endeavor. Belatedly, I now realize that the actual improvement method, be it Six Sigma, business process reengineering, or whatever the latest and greatest method of the day is, may not be nearly as important as we may wish, promote, or posit to think. Rather, the resultant outcome of any performance improvement effort represents the combined effects of:

■ The total capacity of the system
■ The life cycle stage and associated unrealized performance capacity (e.g., available performance improvement potential)
■ The efficacy of the implemented improvement method, technology, or process

We have all heard the saying that "you can't squeeze blood out of a turnip," especially if there is not much blood available to squeeze in the first place. The same holds for performance improvement. You can squeeze (or try to improve) something all you want, but if the potential or capacity is not there, no amount of squeezing, despite associated effort and cost, will produce the desired result. Accordingly, when you think of improving performance, you must consider more than just the applicable or selected improvement method. Rather, your first consideration must always be capacity and available improvement potential because, in the end, it is capacity (or the so-called walls of performance) that actually matter most.

If you have a 1-gallon jug into which you attempt to pour more than 1 gallon of liquids, you can certainly improve your jug-filling technique, but in the end, that improved jug-filling technique will always be limited to only 1 gallon unless you get a bigger jug. As such, when you think about performance you must always consider:

■ The size of the jug (the total performance capacity of the system)
■ The current state of the jug (the amount of realized and remaining unrealized performance capacity)
■ The selected jug-filling technique (the selected performance improvement method)

In the following section, I will briefly explore each of these key factors via an examination of the global production of oil, and examine how, in the end, although advances in technology and process certainly matter, capacity ultimately matters more. Acknowledging such practical capacity-based limitations, a subsequent section will offer some insights into how to more effectively go about the performance improvement process based on earlier discussions of performance modeling and measurement. Finally, I will combine this information in a final practical application section based on the already developed SPOTC performance model from Chapters 5 and 6.

Capacity Matters

Whether describing biological, geological, technological, economic, or just about any other system, life cycle stage and total capacity matter. This is an almost unalterable fact that is often forgotten in our haste to sell a given improvement method, process, or technology. Additionally, capacity is rarely equally distributed within a given population. The study of giant oil fields is a good example of this harsh and unequal reality.

Currently there are some 47,500 known oil fields in the world. Yet despite this large number, only 507 known fields, or slightly more than 1 percent, are currently labeled *giant oil fields*. By definition, a giant oil field is an oil field that will ultimately produce more than 500 million barrels (0.5 Gb) of oil. (As an aside, a barrel of oil contains 42 U.S. gallons, a measure standardized in 1866.) Note that although oil is priced in barrel units, it has not actually been shipped that way since the invention of pipelines and oil tankers.

Giant oil fields, although admittedly tiny in number, are nevertheless disproportionately large in other measures, as depicted in Figure 7.1. According to a recent doctoral dissertation on giant oil fields by Fredrik Robelius of Uppsala University in Sweden, such fields account for over 60 percent of current oil production and some 65 percent of ultimate recoverable oil reserves. Truly, when it comes to oil fields in general and giant oil fields in particular, capacity matters.

The Persian Gulf, for example, is of such vital importance to the world from an energy perspective because it holds 144, or 28 percent, of all known giant oil fields. In fact, fifteen of the twenty largest known giant oil fields in the world, including the Ghawar field (a giant among giants), are found in the Persian Gulf. The Ghawar field, located in Saudi Arabia, was discovered in 1948 with initial production beginning in 1951. Ultimate recoverable reserves are estimated at somewhere between 66 and 150 billion barrels of oil!

As illustrated by the giant oil field example, capacity determines how much blood one can ultimately squeeze out of a turnip or, in this case, how much

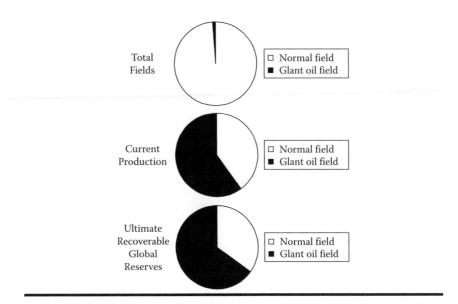

Figure 7.1 Although small in number, the significance of giant oil fields is clearly seen when plotted as a percentage of current production and ultimate recoverable global oil reserves.

oil that can ultimately be pumped out of the ground. Although advances in petroleum-related technology certainly matter, in the end, such advances will always be limited by available capacity or the amount of oil contained in any given field.

To illustrate this limiting reality, Thunder Horse is the largest oil field discovered to date in the deep offshore waters of the Gulf of Mexico. Ultimate recoverable reserves are estimated at 1 billion barrels of oil. Currently, the field is being readied for production in some 6,000 feet of water. Technology needed to discover and produce oil from these water depths is truly mind boggling. But in the end, and despite such amazing technological feats, Thunder Horse is still a 1 Gb field—certainly impressive, but in reality actually rather small in stature among other giant oil fields of the world.

By contrast, fairly crude 1930s' technology was able to discover and produce the East Texas field that contained some 6 Gb of oil. Indeed, over the 10-year period between 1926 and 1936, discoveries made in the oil fields of Texas amounted to almost 20 billion barrels of oil. As illustrated by the incredible accomplishment of Thunder Horse, technology matters, but also illustrated by the developed onshore oil fields of Texas, capacity matters even more.

Indeed, no matter how much improvement technology one applies to Thunder Horse, it will almost certainly never produce as much oil as the East Texas field, and certainly not as much as Ghawar. Why? Because it lacks the requisite capacity. And in the end, it is capacity that truly matters most.

Accordingly, no matter how advanced or effective a proffered improvement method may be, it is ultimately constrained by the total or ultimate capacity of the subject system. Performance walls do exist, and to ignore such realities only invites disappointment and disillusionment. Just as oil fields are constrained by ultimate recoverable reserves, so is any system constrained by some ultimate capacity limit. Yet this constrained reality does not preclude the fact that many systems still possess significant improvement potential as represented by exploitable unrealized performance capacity—a topic to which I turn your attention in the following section.

Realizing Unrealized Performance Capacity

Total performance capacity determines what is *theoretically* possible. Given that you have an abundance of liquid, a 1-gallon jug will theoretically hold 1 gallon. Unrealized performance capacity determines what one has to *realistically* work with. If your 1-gallon jug is half full, then unrealized performance capacity is 0.5 gallon. That 0.5-gallon number represents how much more fluid you can still place in the 1-gallon jug.

As such, *total capacity* sets the walls of performance, *realized capacity* partially fills up the space between those walls, and *unrealized capacity* represents any remaining potential or unfilled space that you might successfully exploit. In real-world systems, unrealized performance capacity is primarily a function of total performance capacity and life cycle stage. Life cycle stage, in turn, normally determines realized performance capacity and remaining unrealized performance capacity or improvement potential.

In Chapter 3, I introduced the concept of a life cycle and its five component stages: birth, growth, maturity, decline, and death. In the early life cycle stage of growth, unrealized performance capacity is, relatively speaking, usually fairly high. Conversely, in later, more mature stages, performance capacity decreases markedly. Figure 7.2 illustrates this differential reality based on life cycle stage via two differing S-shaped curve growth forms.

Figure 7.2(a) represents a system in an obvious early stage of growth. Note that in this instance, the characteristic S-shaped curve is poorly developed. By analogy, one can assume that, relatively speaking, there is still ample unrealized performance capacity to be realized (that is, improved).

Conversely, Figure 7.2(b) represents a fairly mature system, as depicted by an almost complete S-shaped curve form. In this instance, unrealized performance capacity has been almost fully exploited. Irrespective of the selected per-

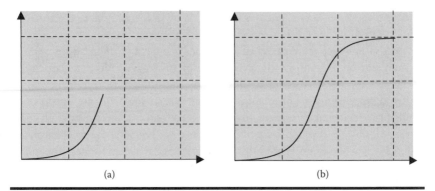

Figure 7.2 Two depictions of life cycle growth at decidedly different stages. In (a), growth is clearly in an early inflationary phase with abundant relative unrealized performance capacity still available. Conversely, (b) depicts a system in a very mature, almost no-growth phase with little, if any, unrealized performance capacity still available.

formance improvement method, there is essentially little unrealized capacity available to be successfully exploited in the system associated with Figure 7.2(b). In such instances, any performance improvement effort will likely be mediocre at best. Accordingly, the ultimate success of any chosen performance improvement method is as much a function of life cycle stage as it is the efficacy of the selected improvement method itself.

Returning to the oil field example, a typical oil-related life cycle includes first oil, buildup, plateau, decline, and abandonment. Note the similarity to the more idealized birth, growth, maturity, decline, and death life cycle stages. In such oil field life cycle scenarios, unrealized performance capacity, or the amount of oil remaining to be produced, is essentially a function of life cycle stage.

Oil production from the North Sea vividly illustrates this sometimes harsh life cycle reality. Consisting of different-sized offshore oil fields, the North Sea area began initial production in 1965. Figure 7.3 plots average daily production as measured by thousand barrels of oil produced daily. Clearly, you can see from Figure 7.3 that oil production has passed its peak and is currently in decline. Figure 7.4 plots cumulative production over the same intervening period, as represented by a moderately well-developed S-shaped growth form.

If you assume for illustrative purposes that the back half of North Sea oil production will look essentially the same as the first half, you can complete the normal curve illustrated in Figure 7.3 with abandonment or final oil production projected to occur in 2034. This mirror-imaging exercise is graphically illustrated in Figure 7.5. Based on Figure 7.5, you can complete your associated cumulative

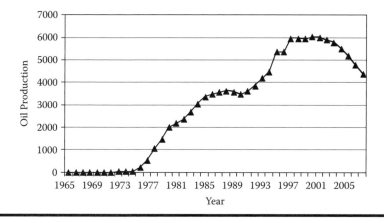

Figure 7.3 A plot of average daily oil production from the North Sea area as measured in thousands of barrels of oil produced daily.

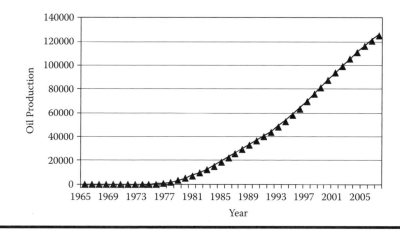

Figure 7.4 The same plot as in Figure 7.3, except in this case cumulative oil production is plotted as a function of time.

frequency curve, as illustrated in Figure 7.6. Note the almost perfect S-shaped curve depicted in Figure 7.6.

In turn, if you take Figures 7.5 and 7.6 and simply divide the curves into quartiles, you see how unrealized performance capacity, represented by remaining oil production levels, decreases through time. This quartering exercise is illustrated in Figure 7.7. Note that both yearly and cumulative production figures are graphed for each quartile. Also note how the depicted normal and S-shaped curves become more normal and S-shaped simply as a function of con-

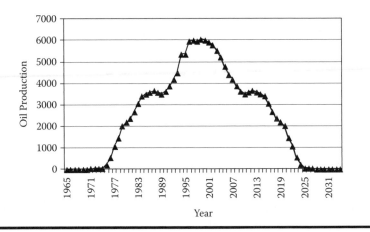

Figure 7.5 A hypothetical complete life cycle depiction of average daily oil production for the North Sea area, developed by extrapolating the front half of the graph plotted in Figure 7.3 to the back half in Figure 7.4. Note the resultant bell-shaped curve.

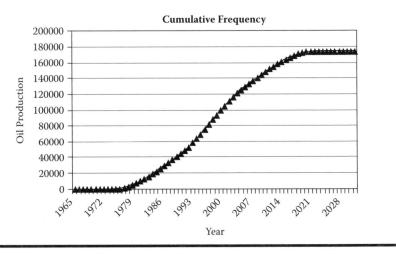

Figure 7.6 A cumulative frequency plot of Figure 7.5. Note the almost perfectly developed S-shaped curve form.

tinued production over time. Also observe how unrealized performance capacity is being increasingly realized or decreased as a function of that same production process over time.

One would certainly expect over the approximate 70-year, first-oil-to-abandonment life cycle illustrated in Figure 7.7, that significant technological advancements occurred, and indeed they did occur. And yet, unfortunately for an ever increasingly energy-thirsty world, such advancements cannot eliminate the inevitability of life cycle aging and the fixed amount of oil that will ultimately be produced from the North Sea area, as illustrated in the plotted graph forms.

This inevitability of life cycle progression, as depicted in the North Sea example, vividly illustrates how increasing amounts of unrealized performance capacity are often realized simply as a function of time. In such life cycle scenarios, death represents the final and ultimate realization of unrealized capacity (it becomes 0 again). Or in performance speak, death implies that there is simply nothing left to improve.

This perhaps grim assessment certainly does not mean that you should not try to improve system performance. But it does mean that you should perhaps be a bit more circumspect in your proposed improvement endeavors. Indeed, it is suggested that your ability to improve performance may not be nearly as related to the nature of the improvement method as people may wish to think. Rather, corresponding differences in performance gains are probably more a function of system life cycle stage than the efficacy of the specific improvement method itself. If this observation is true, then it may be much more difficult to compare differing performance improvement methods than previously thought.

Improvement efforts in an immature system, for example, will most likely result in substantial gains irrespective of the improvement method selected. Conversely, in a more mature system, significant gains are much harder to accrue and, somewhat paradoxically, the efficacy of the improvement method may actually be more important, although resultant gains will likely be less.

Using such a capacity-based vernacular, you can define *performance improvement* as a method, process, or technology for realizing or exploiting unrealized performance capacity. That is, performance improvement is simply a process for filling the unfilled 1-gallon jug!

The goal of any performance improvement effort, therefore, should be to realize unrealized performance capacity in the most efficient and effective manner possible. Yet the actual outcome of such an improvement effort is dependent not only on the efficacy of the selected method itself, but in many situations, is even more dependent on the total capacity and life cycle stage of the system in question, whether that system represents a business process, a human, a horse,

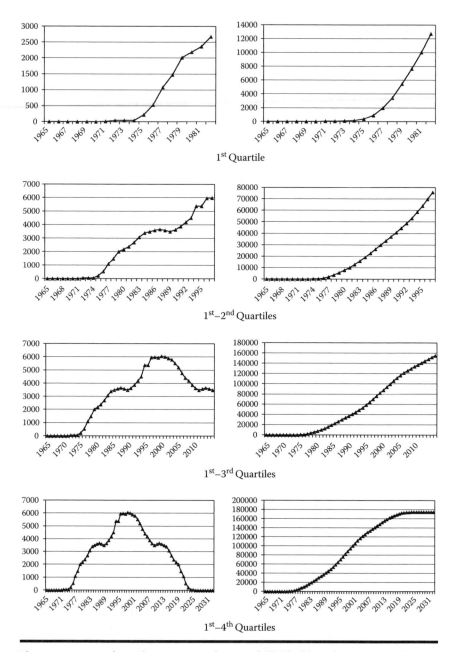

Figure 7.7   Based on Figures 7.5 and 7.6 and divided into four temporal-based quartiles, one can observe the hypothetical progression of North Sea oil production over time. Note how normal and S-shaped curves become more normal and S-shaped as a function of continued production.

or a speed boat. In short, method certainly matters, but capacity (both total and unrealized) ultimately matters more.

The importance of capacity in any performance improvement effort cannot be overstated. In many performance improvement endeavors, a set of baseline (or as-is) measures are taken prior to the start of the improvement process itself. Subsequent after (or post) improvement measures are then collected to calculate overall percent increase in performance as a supposed result of the improvement endeavor. An often overlooked and admittedly more difficult task in such as-is (or baselining) efforts is determining remaining improvement potential (that is, unrealized performance capacity) in the context of current performance levels.

Figure 7.8 plots current performance levels for three abstract systems labeled A, B, and C. As graphically depicted, system A has the highest current performance level, followed by systems B and C, respectively. Note, however, that unrealized performance capacity varies markedly among the three entities, such that C actually has the greatest performance potential, at least theoretically speaking. Although C is currently the poorest performer, it has the greatest improvement potential among the three entities and thus could ultimately become the best performer.

Accordingly, if you expose systems A, B, and C to the exact same improvement method, you would expect that the greatest accruals in improvement would actually occur within system C, the second within B, and the least within A, the current top performer. In this particular instance, the difference in improvement gains has nothing to do with the implemented improvement methodology per se, since the exact same method is used across all three systems. Rather, in this

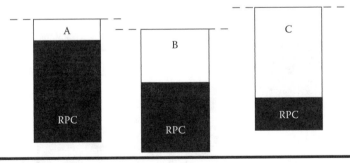

Figure 7.8 **Although current performance as represented by the top of realized performance capacity (RPC) is greatest for System A, ultimate potential performance levels as depicted by the dashed lines are actually greater for System C. Also note the widely differing amounts of unrealized performance capacity (the white portion) available within each system.**

case, improvement gains are solely a function of the amount of available unrealized performance capacity within each system.

In Figure 7.9, I replot the three systems again. Note this time, however, that although system C still has the greatest performance improvement potential on a percentage basis, system C's maximum achievable performance level is now less than that of system A. Although C has the greatest potential gain in performance on an overall percentage basis, system A's total performance (as measured by some outcome Y) is still, and essentially always will be, the greater of the two. Although in such instances performance gains are primarily a function of remaining unrealized performance capacity, ultimate or maximum achievable performance levels are a function of total capacity. As illustrated in Figure 7.9, system A simply has a greater total performance capacity than does system C.

Placing this observation in the context of our discussion of giant oil fields, a 1-billion-barrel Thunder Horse field can never outproduce, in total, a 100-billion-barrel Ghawar oil field, irrespective of how advanced and complex the associated improvement technologies may be. Although this discussion is certainly not meant to dismiss the importance of performance improvement, such efforts must be placed in their proper context. Improvement is important, but it will almost always be restricted or confined within the ultimate performance capacity of the subject system.

Given these expressed realities of improving performance, what is the best way to go about it? In the next section, you will see how returning to your initially created performance model and developed performance measures offers vital insights into the "how to go about it" question.

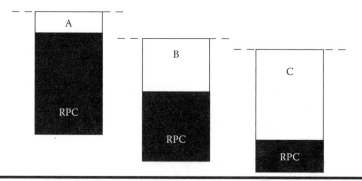

Figure 7.9 Essentially the same graphical depiction as in Figure 7.8. Note, however, that in this instance, System A now has the greatest ultimate performance level even though System C still has the most remaining unrealized performance capacity (shown in white) for subsequent improvement.

Model- and Measurement-Based Performance Improvement

In Chapter 6, I posed the "what to measure" question and answered it by saying that you measure objects previously identified in your developed performance model. Remember that higher-level component objects are essentially performance-related oomph factors that can be further decomposed into a series of mid-level sub-objects and even lower-level elements and sub-elements. Also remember that you can identify three types of performance measures: descriptive, predictive, and prescriptive or diagnostic measures.

It should come as no surprise, then, that when you ask the "What should we improve?" question, the answer is that you should always attempt to improve your previously identified set of objects. You should further use selected and implemented performance measures to better guide and refine your improvement efforts. Accordingly, and as illustrated in Figure 7.10, performance models should drive developed performance measures. In turn, performance measures, especially prescriptive or diagnostic measures, should drive subsequent performance improvement efforts.

If you know, for example, that component object A is an important oomph factor and that measures of component object A indicate poor associated performance levels, then you need to focus your improvement efforts on attempting to improve the performance of component object A. However, such higher-level component object measures may not always precisely identify the exact performance-related problem or answer the "What do we specifically need to improve?" question.

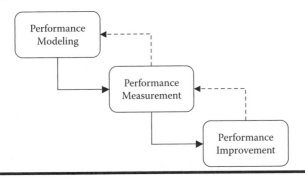

Figure 7.10 As depicted, performance models should always determine what is measured. In turn, performance measures should drive associated performance improvement efforts. Feedback loops (dashed lines) should always be developed and used to improve both performance modeling and performance measurement efforts.

Fortunately, in these situations, mid- and lower-level sub-object- and element-related measures can often assist in better diagnosing and improving performance issues associated with a particular component object. In such instances, you can use your previously developed and model-based performance measurement system to more closely zoom in on a particular performance issue, thus deriving increasingly greater diagnostic and associated prescriptive resolution.

Recall the Human Development Index (HDI) example, where poor life expectancy numbers were primarily caused by higher-than-normal adolescent mortality rates. In turn, these identified higher-than-expected adolescent mortality rates were correlated with a low immunization rate on a per 100,000 population basis. Accordingly, the low immunization rates figure not only helped you diagnose the lower-than-expected life expectancy problem, but also prescribed a specific improvement method: inoculate more adolescent children.

As illustrated by this HDI example, there is often a strong linkage between a constructed performance model and derived measures, and between performance measures and prescribed remedies or selected improvement methods. Indeed, once you know the specifics of what to improve, the "how to improve" question often becomes much more manageable and fairly straightforward. You simply improve, if possible, what the measures prescribe.

In some instances, the "how to improve" question becomes a function of a better selection process. In other instances, it may become an issue of more training, practice, or feedback. At other times, it may require process-specific improvements or the development and implementation of new and innovative cladogenic technologies. Irrespective of the selected how-to method, such improvement efforts should always be driven by what the Y- and x-related measures are attempting to tell you.

It has often been my professional observation that just as many organizations have no real developed process for selecting performance measures (that is, no developed performance model), they also have no real process in place to guide their performance-related improvement efforts. In many instances, I have seen managers randomly solicit performance improvement ideas from employees on a more or less ad hoc basis. Unfortunately, in such instances, there is no process in place for properly selecting, prioritizing, and assessing such collected employee recommendations. Although some very good suggestions may be proffered by this open and certainly more democratic process, acquired good suggestions are unfortunately often lost in a sea of potentially costly and time-consuming non-oomph suggestions.

Conversely, I have observed that organizations who take a more structured and disciplined approach to performance improvement seem to do much better over time. Although admittedly the proposed model-measure-improve performance process depicted graphically in Figure 7.10 comes with no guarantees of success, it is in reality probably about as good of a performance improvement process as there is. This observation seems especially true if organizations take the time to continually refine their developed performance models while continually learning from associated and implemented performance measurement systems and improvement initiatives.

In summary, performance models should drive performance measures. In turn, collected and interpreted performance measures should drive associated performance improvement efforts. Remember, however, that any improvement endeavor will always be bounded by the walls of performance. The good news is that for many systems there is still ample room to successfully realize or maneuver within these defined performance-related boundaries.

Improving SPOTC Performance

What you really need to focus on is improving performance-related objects or previously identified and defined oomph factors. Additionally, well-thought-out and developed diagnostic measures can often identify performance-specific problems and even suggest appropriate improvement-related prescriptive actions. I will illustrate how the use of such prescriptive and diagnostic measures can aid improvement efforts for a final SPOTC-related case study.

In the Chapter 6 case study about the Security Protection Officer Training Competition, we identified specific performance-related problems via differing diagnostic measures for four competing participants labeled A, B, C, and D. Associated diagnostic measures suggested the following:

- Participant A repeatedly experienced speed-related problems with a particular obstacle (a culvert).
- Participant B was a poor pistol shot across all events.
- Participant C continuously had problems hitting a moving target.
- Participant D experienced accuracy-related problems when shooting from certain firing positions.

In each case, affected participants were experiencing a specific skill-based problem to some degree. The question is why? Possible causes may include the following:

- Participants have not adequately acquired a particular skill (such as learning how to properly shoot a pistol).
- Participants have not had an adequate number of practice trials (such as shooting from a particular firing position).

- Participants simply do not have the capacity or potential to perform a particular skill at such competitive levels, possibly due to some physically limiting factor (such as a very large person who simply cannot scramble through a long culvert as fast as a smaller person).
- Although participants actually do have the requisite skills, their performance is adversely affected by other intervening factors, such as stress or fatigue.

What we often want to know in such cases is where an individual is on a particular life-cycle-related skill curve. Skill development very much parallels the standard S-shaped curve growth model: in the beginning, steep gains in improvement are often realized with relatively few practice trials. Despite such continuing and ever-increasing practice sessions over time, however, gains in performance normally begin to slow markedly, eventually reaching a little or no continued improvement–related asymptote (or wall).

Think back to increases in life expectancy as a function of healthcare spending. Small investments resulted in big initial gains, whereas increasing expenditures resulted in ever-decreasing gains until little or no improvements were observed in life expectancy. This same rapid to slow gain to no gain performance phenomenon occurs with skill acquisition as well, irrespective of an ever-increasing number of accrued practice sessions. As such, in any skill development effort, all individuals eventually reach their own particular performance walls simply due to innate physical or mental limitations. Admittedly and fortunately, some individuals encounter such walls much later than others. Given enough time, however, genetic-controlled nature ultimately prevails over effort-based nurture!

Accordingly, we must ascertain in our SPOTC-related example whether such walls have been reached by our four participants, or if there is still ample improvement space available via practice and associated coaching. Remember that there are always limitations at both the system level (*Homo sapiens*) and the individual level. What we need to determine for each individual, then, is whether we are dealing with a nature or nurture issue. All too often, for example, organizations are quick to prescribe more training as a performance-related solution. Yet what organizations often fail to do in such instances is accurately determine whether it is really a training problem, and if it is, do the individuals have the available capacity to even be successfully trained?

Returning to our four SPOTC participants, biology (or in this case, size) is working against Participant A when it comes to rapidly crawling through a lengthy culvert. Although continued conditioning may help Participant A, it is doubtful that increased conditioning will ultimately render significant increases in performance. In this instance, nature may be the ultimate controlling factor.

Conversely, perhaps Participant B has acquired some very bad shooting habits with a handgun. Retraining, along with continued and correct practice, may promote significant gains in shooting accuracy in this example.

For Participant C, who seems to have trouble hitting a moving target, a quick check finds that he normally practices with only fixed targets. In this case, more practice shooting at moving targets may result in significant gains in performance.

Finally, Participant D lacks requisite upper body and hand strength to accurately aim, hold, and fire a weapon from certain unsupported firing positions. Accordingly, strength conditioning could be the proper performance improvement antidote in this case.

The probability of these suggested solutions resulting in significant gains in performance is predicated on the fact that available improvement space actually exists. Although training in many instances certainly matters, in the end, capacity matters more. Accordingly, the real and more radical challenge in any improvement endeavor is figuring out how to successfully break through the so-called walls or limitations of performance, thus reaching ever new performance heights.

Summary

Your ability to successfully improve performance is primarily a function of (1) total performance capacity, (2) life cycle stage and associated unrealized performance improvement potential, and (3) the efficacy of the selected improvement method. Although the improvement method matters, capacity and life cycle stage often matter more. Your ability to improve performance, therefore, may not be nearly as related to the nature of the improvement method as you may wish to think. Rather, differences in gains in performance are probably more a function of system life cycle stage than the efficacy of the improvement method itself. As such, it may be much more difficult to compare differing performance improvement methods than previously thought. This observation seems especially true when we attempt to compare a performance improvement endeavor in an immature versus mature system.

Yet despite such limitations, performance improvement efforts in some systems can accrue substantial gains over time. Irrespective of realized performance improvement potential, however, any improvement effort should be driven by linked performance measures that in turn are driven by a previously developed and constantly refined performance model. Accordingly, a model-measure-improve performance triad should form the foundational basis for any improvement endeavor.

Chapter 8

Performance

A Summary

And that's it! I hope that over the previous chapters, pages, and embedded figures, you have come to view performance a bit differently. Just as you can learn a great deal by reading a book, so can authors learn much while writing one. Often, during the writing process, new insights are gained that force a writer to rethink the initial premise.

Personally, while writing *The Performance Paradox*, I have gained a new appreciation for the so-called limits (or walls) of performance and the reality of resultant S-shaped performance curves. This newly acquired knowledge will certainly make me more circumspect in what I promise future clients in terms of performance outcomes. I have also come to appreciate the importance of oomph factors and performance models, and the associated value of performance measures, especially diagnostic or prescriptive measures. Finally, I have become captivated by the role of innovation and how new innovations may begin the performance improvement process anew. Yet I also realize that despite the introduction of a new innovation, resultant performance gains will mostly accrue in an incremental fashion, one small gain at a time.

I would like to end this performance-related discourse, then, with a quick review of key points captured in each chapter's summary. This is a set of intermediary points that will leave you with both answers and questions, and perhaps will even stimulate a new curiosity, a curiosity that will inspire you to continue to seek what is true and to better understand how performance does and does not improve.

To *perform* means to initiate and execute a set of actions (an activity). The translation of these actions into an actual result, outcome, or accomplishment is termed *performance*. Associated performance-related actions are thus the means, whereas the accomplishment is the end result. Performance, therefore, represents something tangible—an end. It is defined as an outcome, accomplishment, or result.

A performance outcome is commonly expressed with the letter Y. In turn, those factors or variables that supposedly cause or contribute to outcome Y are often designated with an x. Y thus represents the *end*, and x the *means* to a derived performance outcome. Based on these Y and x symbols, you can write a simple formula describing performance. In short, performance outcome Y is a function of variable set x. This is often portrayed by the formula $Y = f(x)$. Developing a $Y = f(x)$ model is key to successfully understanding, measuring, and improving performance.

There are three basic types of x factors: (1) those that significantly affect performance outcome Y in a *positive* manner, (2) those that significantly affect performance outcome Y in a *negative* manner, and (3) those that have little or no effect on outcome Y. It is always critical to identify those few key x factors that truly affect outcome Y—those key factors that have significant oomph value.

Performance improves in a rather predictable fashion irrespective of venue, industry, business, or just about anything else. Initial slow growth often gives way to rapid growth, only to be eventually replaced once again by slow growth that ultimately ends in no growth. This slow growth, fast growth, slow growth, no growth cycle results in a characteristic S-shaped curve that represents a very visual and almost universal symbol for cumulative life cycle growth.

The fact that there are limits to actual gains in performance means that every performance system has a certain *total performance capacity* that controls ultimate growth. Based on life cycle position and theoretical capacity thresholds, *unrealized performance capacity* can vary widely between and among differing performance systems. Accordingly, in some instances, performance improvement potential is quite limited. In other instances, however, significant improvement potential may exist. Understanding the amount of improvement potential available in any given system not only better guides related performance improvement efforts, but also assists in setting more realistic improvement expectations among vested stakeholders.

Performance gains accrue primarily through a series of incremental Type I innovations within a particular lineage. Such innovations commonly have a fairly high initial improvement frequency at the beginning of a new lineage, often exhibiting a positive exponent increase with compound growth (the steep part of the S-curve). Within this Type I innovation–dominated high-frequency phase, however, individual performance gains generally remain relatively small.

Yet in some instances, fairly substantial within-lineage performance gains occur as well.

Given enough time, Type I innovations almost always eventually stagnate and begin to stall out. Such slowing in incremental improvement frequency and resultant gains in performance results in a curve that begins to flatten abruptly, representing now a negative exponent increase and the initial formation of the top of the S. In this more mature phase, few performance gains accrue and the lineage becomes more or less stagnant, at least from a performance growth perspective.

In such mature growth situations, performance gains seem to be able to begin anew only through the introduction of a new innovation and the resultant creation of a new lineage. The start of this new lineage in turn often leads to a new round of incremental Type I innovations that in turn continue to accrue gains in performance. Accordingly, Type II, III, or IV innovations seem to beget Type I innovations. Type I innovations in turn result in incremental gains in performance (at least for a while).

A model represents an *abstraction* of the real world (that is, a *target system*). Any modeling effort attempts to use the familiar to understand the unfamiliar. An effective way to build a model is via *decomposition*. Using an object-oriented language and approach, a *global model* is decomposed into *component objects*. Component objects in turn are decomposed into *sub-objects*. Sub-objects can be further decomposed into *elements* and *sub-elements*.

Developed models can be either generic or specific in origin and application. A *performance model* is a generic or specific model that attempts to identify the key component objects, sub-objects, elements, and sub-elements, and their associated interactions and interrelations that affect or determine some wanted or unwanted performance outcome Y.

A relatively easy-to-follow method for developing a performance model involves six iterative steps:

1. Developing an initial understanding of the subject domain to be modeled
2. Identifying outcome $Y(s)$
3. Observing and measuring the particular domain or real world to be modeled
4. Identifying critical x's
5. Decomposing identified x's into component objects, sub-objects, elements, and sub-elements (if needed)
6. Identifying interrelations and interactions between and among the identified objects in terms of a developed model-related rule set

Measurement involves ascertaining the size, amount, or degree of something. Performance measurement attempts to measure or ascertain either the ends or outcomes of performance (value *Y*), and the means (*x* factors) that affect such outcomes. There are three basic types of performance measures: descriptive, predictive, and prescriptive measures. Note that, in some instances, and depending on how such measures are graphically displayed, the same measure may serve all three functions.

A *descriptive measure* describes what is happening or has happened. Such measures commonly depict a specific outcome and are often used to trend a particular phenomenon over time from a historical perspective. *Predictive measures* are used to infer the future. They attempt to predict what *may* happen but to date has not happened. Finally, *prescriptive measures* are useful in diagnosing and sometimes improving performance-related problems. Ideally, prescriptive measures answer the question of what can (and can't) we do to improve performance.

Performance models should drive selected performance measures. Accordingly, what should be measured are model-based objects that represent important performance oomph factors. Just as performance models via decomposition have greater in-depth granularity, associated performance measurement systems via the same parallel decomposition process have greater diagnostic and prescriptive resolution.

The ability to successfully improve performance is primarily a function of (1) total performance capacity, (2) life cycle stage and associated unrealized performance improvement potential, and (3) the efficacy of the selected improvement method. Although method matters, capacity and life cycle stage often matter more. As such, the ability to improve performance may not be nearly as related to the nature of the improvement method as people may wish to think. Rather, differences in gains in performance are probably more a function of system life cycle stage than the efficacy of the improvement method itself. Therefore, it may be much more difficult to compare differing performance improvement methods than previously thought. This observation seems especially true when you attempt to compare a performance improvement endeavor in an immature versus mature system.

Yet despite such limitations, performance improvement efforts in some systems can accrue substantial gains over time. Irrespective of realized performance improvement potential, however, any improvement effort should be driven by linked performance measures that in turn are driven by a previously developed and constantly refined performance model. In summary, a model-measure-improve performance triad should always form the foundational basis for any improvement endeavor.

Glossary

Anagenesis. A single lineage undergoing incremental change.

Architecture. The organizational structure of the major components comprising a system and the parameters or rules under which they operate.

Artifact. The fundamental unit of study in the made world.

Asymptote. A straight line that is the limiting value of a curve; a performance barrier, limit, or wall.

Bell-shaped curve. Also called a normal curve, the symmetrical curve of a normal distribution.

Cladogenesis. The division or split of a single lineage into another lineage.

Component. A physically distinct portion of a product that embodies a core design concept.

Component objects. Higher-level constituents of a model.

Correlation. A measure of the relation between two or more variables.

Correlation coefficient. A statistical expression of correlation ranging from −1.00 to +1.00.

Cumulative threat. The sum of local risks present in a given area.

Declarative knowledge. "About" knowledge or "knowing that."

Decomposition. The process of breaking something down into its component elements or simpler constituents.

Descriptive measure. A type of performance measure that describes what is and has happened.

Diffusion. The process in which an innovation is communicated through certain channels over time among the members of a social system.

Elements. Lower-level constituents of a model.

Form. The distinct shape or look of a technological object.

Human Development Index (HDI). A summary measure of human development.

Innovation. The successful exploitation of new ideas.

Innovation adopter. Someone who has made a conscious decision or choice to make full use of an innovation as the best course of action.

Lagging indicator. A descriptive performance measure that measures what has happened.

Leading indicator. A predictive performance measure that attempts to infer or extrapolate into the future.

Life cycle. A representation of growth rate as a function of time; often divided into five stages (birth, growth, maturity, decline, and death).

Lineage. A lineal descent from a common source.

Logistic function. A mathematical function derived from a law that states the rate of growth is proportional to the amount of growth already accomplished and the amount of growth remaining to be accomplished.

Logistics productivity. The amount of cargo that can be transported as measured by tons of material transported per day.

Mean. A simple average, equals the sum of all values divided by the number of values.

Measurement. Ascertaining the size, amount, or degree of something.

Measures of central tendency. Commonly expressed by mean, mode, and median, these are measures referring to the location of the middle or center of a distribution.

Median. The halfway point in a group of numbers.

Mission load. An expression of tons per sortie.

Mode. The most common or frequently occurring value of a group of values or numbers.

Model. An abstraction of the real world.

Model system. A representation of something that we do understand or at least partially understand.

Modeling. A tool used to make sense of something that we do not understand in terms of something that we do understand.

Negative correlation. A relationship between two numbers such that as one variable's value tends to increase, the other variable's value tends to decrease.

Normal curve. *See* bell-shaped curve.

Objects. Elemental components of a model.

Paradox. An opinion or statement that is contrary to commonly accepted wisdom. A declaration or proposition that at first may seem to be absurd or self-contradictory, but in reality expresses a factual truth.

Perform. To initiate and execute a set of actions; an activity.

Performance. An actual outcome, accomplishment, or result.

Performance improvement. A method, process, or technology for realizing or exploiting unrealized performance capacity.

Performance measurement. Ascertaining either the ends or outcomes of performance and the means or variables (x) that affect such outcomes.

Performance measurement system. The collection, synthesis, delivery, and graphical display of performance measures.

Performance metric. A specific performance measure.

Performance model. A model that attempts to identify the key component objects, sub-objects, elements, and sub-elements and their associated interactions and interrelations that drive or determine some wanted or unwanted performance outcome *Y.*

Performance paradox. A paradox that refers to what does and does not drive performance or what does and does not result in a result.

Performance statement. A succinct summary of those key factors that truly drive organizational success.

Positive correlation. A relationship between two numbers such that as one variable's value tends to increase, the other variable's value also tends to increase.

Predictive measure. A performance measure used to infer the future or extrapolate from one measure to another.

Prescriptive measure. A performance measure useful in diagnosing and sometimes improving performance-related problems.

Procedural knowledge. "How to" knowledge.

Realized performance capacity (RPC). Performance capacity that has already been attained or realized in any system.

Risk. The probability and severity of a single occurrence of harm.

S-shaped curve. A representation of cumulative life cycle growth or frequency that results in the shape of an S when plotted graphically.

Sub-elements. The lowest-level constituent of a model.

Sub-objects. Mid-level constituents of a model.

Target system. What we do not understand but want to understand.

Total performance capacity (TPC). The ultimate or maximum performance level that a system can potentially attain.

Type I innovation. Represents a minor or incremental change in both form and internal components.

Type II innovation. Represents a significant change in form but only an incremental change in internal components.

Type III innovation. Represents a significant change in internal components but only an incremental or minor change in form.

Type IV innovation. Represents significant changes in both form and internal components.

Unrealized performance capacity (UPC). The remaining capacity that has not been attained in a system and is thus still unrealized.

x. A common representation of a variable that affects a performance outcome. The means of performance.

Y. A common representation of a performance outcome. The ends of performance.

$Y = f(x)$. A commonly used performance formula indicating that outcome Y is a function (f) of variable set x.

Bibliography

Anonymous. 2004. Anti-ship warfare and molotov cocktails at the Siege of Acre, 1190 (trans. Jamestown Staff). *Terrorism Monitor* 2(9).

Bapat, S. 1994. *Object-oriented networks: Models for architecture, operations, and management.* Englewood Cliffs, NJ: Prentice Hall.

Basalla, G. 1989. *The evolution of technology.* Cambridge, UK: Cambridge University Press.

Berri, D. J., Schmidt, M. B., and Brook, S. L. 2006. *The wages of wins.* Stanford, CA: Stanford Business Books.

Blumberg, M., and Pringle, C. D. 1982. The missing opportunity in organizational research: Some implications for a theory of work performance. *Academy of Management Review* 7:560–69.

Boot, M. 2006. The paradox of military technology. *The New Atlantis*, Fall 2006, pp. 13–31.

Clark, K. B. 1985. The interaction of design hierarchies and market concepts in technological evolution. *Research Policy* 14:235–51.

Costas, B. 2000. *Fair ball: A fan's case for baseball.* New York: Broadway Books.

Cuny, F., with Hill, R. B. 1999. *Famine, conflict, and response: A basic guide.* Bloomfield, CT: Kumarian Press.

Fiedrich, F., Gehbauer, F., and Rickers, U. 2000. Optimized resource allocation for emergency response after earthquake disasters. *Safety Science* 35:41–57.

Franke, W. W., and Berendonk, B. 1997. Hormonal doping and androgenization of athletes: A secret program of the German Democratic Republic government. *Clinical Chemistry* 43:1262–79.

Gale, T., and Eldred, J. 1996. *Getting results with the object-oriented enterprise model.* New York: SIGS Books.

Gennaro, V. 2007. *Diamond dollars—The economics of winning in baseball.* Hingham, MA: Maple Street Press LLC.

Gilbert, T. F. 1978. *Human competence: Engineering worthy performance.* New York: McGraw-Hill.

Gould, S. J. 1996. *Full house.* New York: Three Rivers Press.

Hammer, M., and Champy, J. 1993. *Reengineering the corporation—A manifesto for business revolution.* New York: Harper Business.

Harbour, J. L. 1997. *The basics of performance measurement.* New York: Productivity Press.

163

Harbour, J. L., and Blackman, H. S. 2006. Innovation: The other 'I' word associated with performance. *Performance Improvement* 45:24–29.

Harbour, J. L., and Marble, J. L. 2005. How performance improves. *Performance Improvement* 44:14–19.

Hargadon, A. 2003. *How breakthroughs happen: The surprising truth about how companies innovate.* Boston: Harvard Business School Press.

Henderson, R. M., and Clark, K. B. 1990. Architectural innovation: The reconfiguration of existing product technologies and the failure of established firms. *Administrative Science Quarterly* 35:9–30.

Hollinger, J. 2002. *Pro basketball prospectus 2002.* Washington, DC: Brassey's Sports.

Jaruzelski, B., Dehoff, K., and Bordia, R. 2005. The Booz Allen Hamilton Global Innovation 1000: Money isn't everything. *Strategy + Business*, no. 41, winter.

Johnson, A. 2007. Amid drug-industry crunch, Lipitor pioneer gets laid off. *Wall Street Journal*, December 11, pp. A1, A24.

Keri, J., ed. 2006. *Baseball between the numbers.* New York: Basic Books.

Kolata, G. 2007. Bigger is better, except when it is not. *New York Times,* September 27, pp. E1, E7.

Levin, R. C., Mitchell, G. J., Volcker, P. A., and Will, G. F. 2000. *The report of the independent members of the commissioner's blue ribbon panel on baseball economics.* A study commissioned by Major League Baseball.

Levinson, M. 2006. *The box: How the shipping container made the world smaller and the world economy bigger.* Princeton, NJ: Princeton University Press.

Levitt, S. D., and Dubner, S. J. 2006. *Freakonomics.* New York: HarperCollins.

Lewis, M. 2004. *Moneyball.* New York: W. W. Norton & Company.

McAslan, A., and Feigenbaum, K. 2000. International standards for personal protective equipment. *Journal of Mine Action*, version 4.2, June.

McClosky, D. 1998. *The rhetoric of economics.* 2nd ed. Madison, WI: University of Wisconsin Press.

Mitchell, G. J. 2007. *Report to the commissioner of baseball of an independent investigation into the illegal use of steroids and other performance enhancing substances by players in Major League Baseball.* DLA Piper US LLP Report, commissioned March 30, 2006, by the commissioner of Major League Baseball. 409 pp.

Pfeffer, J., and Sutton, R. I. 2006. *Hard facts, dangerous half-truths and total nonsense: Profiting from evidence-based management.* Boston: Harvard Business School Press.

Powers, S. K., and Howley, E. T. 2007. *Exercise physiology: Theory and application to fitness and performance.* 6th ed. New York: McGraw Hill.

Reason, J. T. 1997. *Managing the risks of organizational accidents.* Aldershot, UK: Ashgate Publishing Ltd.

Robelius, F. 2007. Giant oil fields—The highway to oil. PhD dissertation, University of Uppsala, Sweden.

Rogers, E. M. 2003. *Diffusion of innovations.* 5th ed. New York: Free Press.

Scales, R. H. 2005. Urban warfare: A soldier's view. *Military Review,* January–February, pp. 9–18.

Tango, T. M., Lichtman, M. G., and Dolphin, A. E. 2007. *The book—Playing the percentages in baseball.* Dulles, VA: Potomac Books.

U.S. Department of Education. 2007. *Effectiveness of reading and mathematics software products: Findings from the first student cohort.* Report to Congress.

U.S. General Accounting Office. 1997. *Operation Desert Storm: Evaluation of the air campaign.* Report to the Ranking Minority Member, Committee on Commerce, House of Representatives.

Woods, D. 2003. Creating foresight: How resilience engineering can transform NASA's approach to risky decision making. Testimony on the future of NASA for the Committee on Commerce, Science and Transportation, John McCain, chair, October 29.

Work, G., and Balmforth, A. 1993. Using abstraction to build standardized components for enterprise models. In *Proceedings of the 1993 Software Engineering Standards Symposium*, 154–62. Los Alamitos, CA: IEEE Computer Society Press.

Index